Praise for *Suck It, Wonder Woman!*

"An entertaining and refreshing celebration of feminity."
—Venus Zine

"Our favorite nerd-approved goddess."　　　—*Maxim*

"*Suck it, Wonder Woman!* is a fun, quick, entertaining, and heartfelt read."　　　—*The Daily Loaf*

"Die-hard Munn fans will revel in their geek goddess's tome."
—*Time Out New York*

"Turn to page 92 now!"　　　—Garry Shandling

"A book only Olivia Munn could write. Better read it now; everyone'll be talking about it tomorrow."　　　—Stan Lee

"This book so good. You buy now. Okay, bye."
—Olivia's mom

"If *Citizen Kane* were a book, this would be it."
—Jon Favreau

"She's part Asian! And I like sushi."　　　—Masi Oka

"This book confirms why Olivia has garnered a massive supportive following—she's fearless, honest, relatable, and truly funny."　　　—Elijah Wood

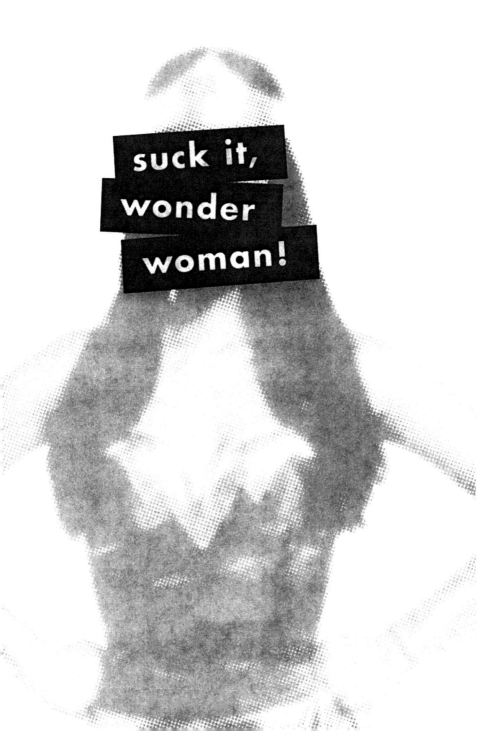

it, er n!

The Misadventures of a Hollywood Geek

Olivia Munn

with Mac Montandon

St. Martin's Press
New York

SUCK IT, WONDER WOMAN! Copyright © 2010 by Olivia Munn with Mac Montadon. All rights reserved. Printed in the United States of America. For information, address St. Martin's Press, 175 Fifth Avenue, New York, N.Y. 10010.

www.stmartins.com

Book design by Jonathan Bennett with Rich Arnold

The Library of Congress has cataloged the hardcover edition as follows:

Munn, Olivia, 1980–
    Suck it, Wonder Woman! : the misadventures of a Hollywood geek /
Olivia Munn, with Mac Montadon.—1st ed.
      p. cm.
    ISBN 978-0-312-59105-2
    1. Munn, Olivia, 1980– 2. Actors—United States—Biography. 3.
Television personalities—United States—Biography. I. Title.
    PN2287.M797 A3 2010
    791.450/28092 B—dc22

                                                        2010013036

ISBN 978-0-312-58376-7 (trade paperback)

First St. Martin's Griffin Edition: July 2011

P1

I'm dedicating this book

to everyone who's ever been mean to me. From family members to girls at school to boyfriends who cheated on me. If you weren't such jerks, I never would've developed such a tough skin to handle Hollywood and be where I'm at today.

So, **thanks for being such assholes!**
I wouldn't have a book deal without you! Cheers!

table of contents

suck it, wonder woman!

introduction

Yeah, so I wrote a book.

I know everyone thinks they have a book in them and that one day they will totally write it and it will be great, but that's not true. For one thing, writing a book is hard as shit. And writing a book that is interesting and entertaining is doubly hard as shit. Plus— who's to say if anyone will give two shits? Ya know?

Now, I'm not saying I'm so great and so interesting, I'm just saying I wrote this book. Tough to argue with that! And while I generally worry that I might be doing a terrible job on stuff and am more likely to suck than to rule when I first try any given thing, I have to say, I gave this book my best shot, with absolute honesty. I hope you agree, but if you don't, that's cool. I'll try better the next time!

*   *   *

I'm not sure many people know that I had a fairly unusual childhood and upbringing. It was the sort of childhood that makes you either desperate and suicidal, or makes you see the humor in almost every situation. I chose laughs.

My mom's parents were Chinese but they moved to Vietnam before she was born. She had eight siblings and my grandfather had a successful bricklaying business. During the Vietnam war, my grandfather was able to pay off the Communists to help his family escape to America. My grandmother and her nine children took a boat to the Philippines and then a plane ride to Oklahoma. Why Oklahoma? Because the only American they knew was a man named Gary, who lived in Oklahoma and offered to help them out any way he could. (Oh, Fun Fact about Gary? This is so crazy. I knew him my whole life and he was like an uncle. A few years ago, there was a really bad winter in Oklahoma, and a lot of homes were damaged. So instead of waiting for insurance to come out and assess his damage, 60-something-year-old Gary climbs onto his roof, steps on his skylight, falls through and is speared by all the falling glass. He lies there dead for a couple of days before anyone finds him. I know! So crazy. All these years, I bet he never thought he'd go out like that. That was an awesome story, you're welcome. But back to this book!) So my mom and her family moved to Oklahoma in the

1970s to attend good schools. Good, Christian schools in Oklahoma.

Now, there's something I should clarify to all you non-Asians reading this. There are two types of Asians. The ones who are quiet, polite, organized and laugh with their hand over their mouths. And then there are the other Asians—the really loud, insane messy ones who hit their kids and yell even when they're just talking about the weather. My family is comprised of loud-ass Asians. The men have serious aversions to shirt wearing—it's like their bodies literally will not allow their hands to go above their head to put on a shirt. It's amazing. And the women scream, hit their kids, and address all white people as "Hey, lady! . . . Hey, you! . . . Hey, lady! . . . Hey, you!"

You know the *Joy Luck Club*? The women in my family should form a new club—The Oh Shit You Some Crazy Asian Lady Club.

I mean that in a nice way and wouldn't want to change them at all. The truth is that as crazy as they can be, they are also wonderful and loving people—so wonderful, infact, that they probably won't kill me for everything I am about to say and for my riffing on their foibles.

I'll just run it down for you: One aunt has a daughter who is an ex-beauty queen and a son who lived in his room for three years as a shut-in. Like, he wouldn't come out ever. He was just in there, not talking to anyone, playing

World of Warcraft or whatever. He had my aunt's credit card to order food to live on. My mom once asked my aunt how she knew he was even alive, and my aunt answered that sometimes she would see a light go on or off. That was her only sign of life, or so she speculates, a light switch. Eventually she lured him out and drove him to MY MOM'S house in Oklahoma and told my mom to deal with him. It was crazy! I don't think the treatment took, as he stayed with my mom for a year before going back home because he refused to go to school or say please or thank you or be . . . normal.

This same aunt—fun thing about her—I'm pretty sure is a hoarder. She once bought like thousands of dollars worth of rice cookers because they were on sale. She can't control herself around a good deal. Or a bad one. She once bought out a store of its swing gliders and made everyone in the family throw away their beds to sleep on their very own, individual swing glider.

Another aunt married a guy who makes decent money, so now there is nothing for her to do but go to the gym and take long showers there. Why? I think she does that to save money. In the past, when she came to my mom's house for dinner, she brought a plastic bag and took fruits and vegetables my mom just bought. According to family lore, she hides food under her bed so her kids won't find it. The good food. The other food she keeps in the fridge for her kids to eat. What kind of food, you ask? Like, spaghetti with tuna fish, marinara sauce and carrots—all in one big pot. That way they don't have to eat *her* good food and she doesn't have to cook for a week. When her kids were young she found a way to make cash off of them. She offered to pay them for chores but when they didn't do them to her satisfaction she deducted the amount from the ledger, so at the end the month her kids *would owe her!* All kidding aside, I have to hand it to her; that would be kind of a genius financial strategy. She might have a future at Goldman Sachs.

One aunt dresses in short shorts, hot pants and tank tops because she's desperate to look young. One day she decided she wanted to change her name to Britney. Yes, just like Britney Spears. "Call me Brit-UH-Knee," she told everyone at the gym. "Call me Brit-UH-Knee, because I Brit-UH-Knee Spears, okay?" Once one of her gym buddies called the house asking for Britney and her husband slammed down the phone. "Hey," my aunt pleaded. "Hey, that was my friend. Let me talk to my friend. You tell them I am Brit-UH-Knee."

Then there's the Doc. The Doc is my aunt who is a successful radiologist. And that's another thing about my family—they all possess the clichéd Asian drive to succeed, so they all are super-educated and some of them have done really well in their chosen professions. A few of

them are doctors and engineers. Doc is so talented she even taught her cats to pee on the toilet.

One other aunt is always in pajamas, and usually I think I can make out some sort of juice or soda or stain all over it. And everyone acts like she's "simple," but she's not and she loves her garage sales. It seems like all she does all day is drive around in a pickup truck going to garage sales. So whatever new thing you have, whatever you just bought, she could've gotten it for you cheaper. Here is a an invented—but not totally off base—exchange:

This aunt: Hey, nice MacBook. Where'd you get it?

Me: Um, the Mac store.

Aunt: How much did you pay?

Me: I don't know, about $2,000 or so.

Aunt: Oh really? You know, I could buy at garage sale for one dollah.

But I have to say, as crazy as my family is, I am very proud of what they've done. They spent all their money to come to America for a better life. All nine children graduated from college. And some have gone on to have their own radiology practices, or they've worked for NASA, or have been a top engineer for Ford, and they've become teachers and parents. I am so very proud of that. Yes, they're crazy, but who isn't? I think it's much better to acknowledge and embrace and, damn I say, celebrate the craziness, than to pretend it doesn't exist or try to convince people my family is something "perfect." Because honestly, the craziness is kind of fun and made me the person I am today.

So, yes, there has always been a lot of yelling in my family. And since my mom remarried an Air Force guy, we've always moved around a lot, too. I think those two factors had a definite effect on me growing up, and to this day, I've looked for shelter and found solace among the quiet and the nerdy. I am a misfit myself and I have always seemed to get along with misfits. And, as I discuss in the pages of this book, I was just lucky that wherever I've been—Oklahoma, Japan, Hollywood—there has been a nerd family willing to take me into their fold.

I think I was raised in a way that was not like everyone else—part Chinese, part white, part Air Force brat, and all geek all the time. The geeks who took me in showed me the many joys of *Tetris*, *Super Mario Brothers*, *Dungeons & Dragons,* and much, much more—they may have saved my life in the process. Or, at the very least, they saved what is left of my sanity. Which is good because then I was able to use that leftover sanity to help me write my book, which, again, I hope you will really like because it doesn't suck and it has a lot of pictures. Some of them were made by my fans who are, no joke, the best fans in the world. Just ask them.

★   ★   ★

Last thing for now—I realize I've talked a little shit about my family here but I hope you realize that when it comes down to it—I wouldn't trade them in for any family in the world. Except maybe the Kennedys because—fuck, the Kennedys! I mean, I would *love* a family compound and to ask people year-round where they "summer"!

No, really, without my family this book would not have been possible at all—so if you hate it, blame them.

chapter one
ruff love

For some reason,

when I was thirteen years old, I thought it would be really neat to wear only clothes that were Disney themed. Fucking everything. My preferred outfit: Mickey Mouse shirts, socks and hair clips, finished off with blindingly white Keds sneakers. Sexy, I know. (Note: If you're a preteen kid about to move to a brand-new school in *a completely different country* it is fate that you're reading this right now—put down the Donald Duck shirt and pick up a gun! Trust me, it will only end badly.)

From the moment I sat in my first-period class on the very first day at my new military school in Japan, I knew things were gonna be bad. There was a group of girls sitting in Science staring me down and whispering amongst themselves. I could make out a little of it:

> "Who does she think she is?"
> And: "Is she really wearing that?"
> Oh, and also: "God, she looks like such a bitch . . . and a slut."

Delightful.

I pretended not to hear and picked a random seat not that far from the cackling cunts. Why did I choose a seat so close to them? I didn't want them to think they were intimidating me. Because the moment they thought they made me feel inferior, it would be over. I decided at that moment that I would never show fear.

The only problem with this plan was that I was scared shitless. I was terrified that no one would like me. That I'd have zero friends—apart from Mickey and Minnie, of course. But these girls apparently saw something that I didn't. Did I have food in my teeth? Were my shorts too tight? Did I pee in them? What the hell were they whispering about?! I calmly excused myself to the restroom to take a quick look.

Standing in front of the mirror I conducted a fast check:

White button-up shirt? Check. Blue Esprit shorts cuffed at the bottom? Check. Mickey Mouse ankle socks with blue rim at the top? Oh, hells yeah, check. Turn around. Yep, there's the whole gang on the back of my shirt: Mickey, Minnie, Goofy, Donald. What could they possibly be saying about what is clearly a genius outfit? I really had no idea. I honestly had no idea that some people might regard me as a preppy douche upon which Walt Disney had hurled massive, Technicolor chunks.

I'd like to say this is where things got better, but that wouldn't make a good story . . . and it wouldn't be true. I made just one friend in six months.

Her name was Eve. She had bangs and one long braid in the back, wore glasses and liked to fold up notes like little origami birds. She would sit with me at lunch and look away helplessly as the other girls would step up one by one and share their one-word descriptions of me.

"Bitch."

"Slut."

"Dickhead."

Dickhead? Seriously? I was only thirteen years old and had never even seen a dick yet.

It was the weirdest thing to be called a slut. I mean, I was only thirteen years old and had never even kissed a boy yet. But, somehow by the grace of God I was, in fact, a slut. And because popular opinion rules in high school,

that's all anyone thought of me. And I got used to being bullied, harassed and having only one friend. At least I had Eve. I can't imagine what it would be like if I didn't have anyone.

But then one day, everything changed for me.

There was a new guy in school and every girl was talking about him. Not because he looked like Brad Pitt, but because we were all so bored. Any new blood was interesting. I'll call him Sam. He was stocky and a little chubby. Had a splotch of acne on his cheeks and floppy blondish brown hair that fell over his eyes. The only other thing I knew about him was that he played soccer. And he wore his backpack straps on both arms—not the one-armed slingover all the

He didn't concentrate too hard and ... yep, heard him die. *Definitely* Mario.

cool kids were doing. Sam gave off an air of not caring at all what people thought of him, whether or not they liked him. He was my hero. I was in love.

I watched him closely for his first week at school. He didn't talk to anyone. He ate lunch by himself and played his Gameboy on a shady patch of grass beside the building. What was he playing? *Tetris*? No—too much finger movement. *Mario*? Possibly. He didn't concentrate too hard and . . . yep, heard him die. Definitely *Mario*.

Sam was awesome at soccer. He was always practicing and could do all these crazy tricks. But the best thing about him? He was always alone. No one seemed to want to talk to him, not even his teammates. Soon word spread through school that everyone thought he was "weird" and "retarded." Wait—so that was why he didn't have any friends?

That's why he didn't have any friends? He was so cute and talented . . . but because he had a little acne and played a Gameboy in his spare time he had some sort of mental retardation? These dumb bitches were as dumb as they were my first day.

One night I made a decision while going through my closet, picking my outfit for the next day—Daisy Duck tank top and jeans: so cute! I decided I would tell Eve to spread the word that I wanted Sam to be my boyfriend. She did; it moved like wildfire or crotch fire or what have you.

The next day it was all anyone could talk about. The school had this low buzzing as its soundtrack: *Olivia likes Sam. Sam likes Olivia. OMG! OMG! OMG!*

So I did the only thing that made sense: I started freaking out. I might have even thrown up on myself. I don't remember. Suddenly there was all this attention on me. Suddenly all those bitches who hated me wanted to quench their gossip thirst, acting like they were my friends just to get the scoop. It was crazy.

"Are you gonna say yes?"

"Are you gonna put out?"

"Are you gonna love him even if he has Down Syndrome?"

Holy. Crap. I freaked. Did I really want him to ask me out? What happens once we're boyfriend/girlfriend? Are we supposed to go to dinners and movies? Get married and have babies? I'm only thirteen! I still wear Minnie Mouse underwear, for God's sake!

I saw Sam part the crowds in the hallway and head straight for my locker. I was so scared. I looked around for someone—anyone!—to talk to. Someone to divert my attention so I could avoid him. I still wanted to be his girlfriend and wanted him to ask me out, but I couldn't stand all the attention.

Now everyone is standing at the sides of the hallway, leaning up against the lockers and watching Sam walking toward me. EVERYONE is looking. So my one and only friend is not by my side but up against a locker with the rest of the herd, staring at the reality show playing out before their eyes. Sam was steps from me, he could reach out and touch me if he wanted . . . We locked eyes, took a breath . . . OMG he's gonna ask me! He starts his first syllable . . . and I turn and walk away.

Wait, what!? Why the hell was I walking away? What's wrong with me? Later I heard he just stood there for a sec-

ond, looking at the empty space where I had been standing. Then he turned around and walked back through the
hallways, the teenagers still parted and backed up against
the lockers, now with their mouths agape and there is a
high-level whisper suffocating the building.

Eve chased after me. She found me crouched down
behind the Health building. She didn't say anything. She
didn't have to. She knew it was just all too much. This sad
spectacle was my life—and I couldn't take it. After several
minutes of thinking about how shitty everything was, about
all my feelings of inadequacy it dawned on me that Sam
must have been feeling really badly, too. My face went
white and my mouth dried up. My inner girlpower forced
me to stand up and go find him.

He was sitting on the soccer field, playing his Gameboy. I walked up and sat down right next to him. No more
prying eyes, no whispers, just us. I saw on the screen that
I was right: *Mario Brothers*. We sat there in silence until the
familiar sound of Mario dying rang across the field. He put
the game down and, without lifting his head to make eye
contact, said, "Will you go out with me?"

I said yes immediately. We sat there for a few more minutes. Then we stood up together, held hands, and walked
back to class.

In just thirty seconds, I was convinced that he was the
best boyfriend ever.

★ ★ ★

A new semester was starting the following week and Sam and I had one class together. He sat behind me in History and everything was great. We were typical, happy thirteen-year-olds who were going out—which meant we never talked or really acknowledged one another. It was wonderful. Everyone just knew we were together.

I was so excited that first day of the new semester. To be honest, I'd never really heard him speak—just the one sentence when he asked me out. We smiled at each other and sat down. I felt content, like everything was going to be okay. I had a friend and a boyfriend and would not have to worry about being attacked anymore. I felt for the first time since moving to this new school, that I would survive.

Ten minutes go by, and all of a sudden Sam grabs my chair, shakes it furiously and screams out what seems to be half of a joke, ". . . AND THEN SHE WAS HIT BY A BUS!" followed by an uproarious laugh, and . . . wait . . . What was that? Was he barking? No. He wasn't barking. He was telling a joke. "Gggrrr . . . Ruff! Ruff!" Umm, yeah. That was a bark. What. The. Fuck?!!!!

I wasn't sure what to do exactly so I did what I was best at back then: I froze. Just like . . . freakin' ice. The Ice Teen Girlie Girl Cometh. Oh yeah, if you freeze, no one can see you. It's common knowledge.

And that was not all—no, that was not all. Because next

came the freak-show grand finale.

"Grrrr . . . ruff ruff ruff ruff ruff ruff . . ." With spit flying from the corner of his mouth like a Saint Bernard.

Umm, yeah. That was definitely a bark. And not some Lassie shit either—this was much closer to Old Yeller, but the Old Yeller after he gets the rabies and they have to kill him with a shotgun . . . yeah, *that* Old Yeller.

I turned around slowly in my seat and looked at him. I was a little afraid but I was also annoyed. Why had he not told me about this sooner? Oh, right, because we had never really spoken to one another. Smooth move, that.

"What are you doing?" I asked, dreading the answer, whatever it was. Sam swallowed hard, took a deep breath and said, "Ggggrr Ruff Ruff! I have Tourette's . . . RUFF!"

God. Damn. Hi, karma, I'm Olivia. I'm sorry for whatever I did in my past life . . . can we move on now?

chapter two
thoughts about my first agent's girlfriend's vagina

When I first moved

out to Los Angeles, I had one sorta-kinda contact. He was a manager. Norm was an old-timey manager—the I'm-Gonna-Make-You-A-Star-Kid type—with a face tight from plastic surgery. I couldn't tell if he was always happy to see me, or in a perpetual state of shock.

I dressed up to go in for my first meeting with him at his office. (Side note: How you dress in L.A. is vastly different from how you dress for important meetings in, say, Oklahoma. In L.A. it's all about looking effortless, like you didn't try. Jeans, flip-flops and a T-shirt. But the jeans should be just tight enough to still be sexy, yet also seem as if you just threw them on. Voila! It should also be noted that I was never alerted to this and so I traipsed into Norm's office in heels and my best dress—they call that your "Sunday Best" where I come from.)

I walked into a room that was covered in magazines, mostly of the tabloid variety. There were posters everywhere of all his clients—in their respective soap operas. Still, I walked in with very high hopes. I hoped that he would sign me as his client, sprinkle me with a pinch of pixie dust, and send me off on my merry way to the Spielbergs' Fourth of July BBQ.

At that moment, all my dreams were riding on this meeting. He was my only connection and only hope. My Obi-Wan Kenobi, if you will (and I think you will).

He checked me out from head to toe and smiled. I think. Okay, no, wait, he just always looked like that—good to know. So he looked me over and . . . went back to reading his magazine. While reading he told me I had to go to an acting class and perform for the teacher. And if the teacher thought I was good enough, he'd represent me. End of meeting!

So I go to this class. Bad news: The teacher said I was too late to be in the acting showcase where agents and managers come and watch actors perform. But, good news! I *could* serve the Chinese food to the agents and managers while they watched the show. I just wanted to see what it was like, so I said yes. Hell, maybe I'd meet an agent in search of an egg roll.

During the performance I snuck in through the back and watched the actors on stage. I saw Norm, with that big maybe smile, sitting in the back. Somehow, despite the end-less grin, he looked very bored.

But then someone came on and caught his eye. She was a former Ms. Texas. Blond and beautiful and couldn't act for shit. I looked over at Marv and noticed that he had really perked up since she came onstage. That's when I realized he would never in a million years represent me. Norm only wanted someone gorgeous who could be plugged into a soap without out any effort at all.

I sat down, defeated. I went back to spooning more and more sweet-and-sour sauce onto plastic plates. The orange goop coagulated in great, gross stains. There is an old adage that says: It is while spooning bright orange sauce onto plas-tic plates that destiny often finds us. Okay, not really. But the truth is, at that moment, a manager approached me. He thought I had a "great look" and wanted me to call him on Monday. OMG. It worked! I didn't have to perform at all, I could just fling plastic soy sauce packets and the universe would take care of the rest. Score!

I called the manager the next day and he quickly set up a meeting with an agent. Soon after that, I walked into the agency, finally dressed down in jeans, tank top and boots. No effort at all. The office was cluttered with magazines—*Vanity Fair*, *US Weekly*, *People*, the works. On the walls were photos of random famous folks: Barbra Streisand, Madonna, Tom

Hanks. Now, I'm no Photoshop genius, but it crossed my mind that the broadly grinning guy standing next to all these celebs was Photoshopped in. Not a great first impression. But I pressed on.

Behind the desk in front of me I saw red hair, a headset and a computer. I couldn't make out what was on the screen, but it must have been important because this agent was screaming at whomever was on the other line. I took a seat and tried desperately to understand his conversation. Was it a big-budget movie he was negotiating for a client? A new TV series? Oh, I know! Tom Cruise was calling and he was creating a show and all of his clients were going to be in it for a million each!

He finished his phone call with sweat drops pooling around his collar, ripped off his headset and threw it onto a pile of magazines. Then he spun around to face me. Smiled, I think.

"I was just trying to get these Madonna tickets," he said. "The seats I wanted were really hard to get, but I fuckin' threw down the cards to get it. Whatever. It's worth it. Hey—what are you doing next week? Wanna house-sit for me?"

Seriously. That's how it went down. I'm sure if any of his clients knew that he spent his days searching online for concert tickets, they would have a better understanding about why their careers had stalled.

I told this maniac that I had absolutely nothing to do and would be totally down for house-sitting. Honestly, I was excited. I didn't know how Hollywood worked. I figured this meant he wanted to represent me. Or at the very least, he'd feel guilty and be unable to reject me because I had done him a big favor. And then he dropped this on me: "Why don't I have you come over early to meet my girl-friend so she feels comfortable around you." Yeah, okay. That made sense. What with the fact that you just asked a complete stranger to watch your house for you.

"Cool. You come over later, then," he said. "And you need some help? I'll represent you."

Yes! Sure, it had started a little strangely with him ignor-ing me for ten minutes while he secured Madonna tickets. But I had an agent! I was so happy! And it was a good agency too, a fine agency. Totally midshelf. The Skyy Vodka of agencies. But for me—brand-new to Hollywood with only theater experience under my belt—it was the best I could do. I could worry about moving up later, right?

I went to his house later that night to meet his fiancée. It was a small house in a busy neighborhood. He didn't own it, he rented—but he had the pride of an owner. He kept saying things like, "Isn't it like a spa in here? It's so serene and peaceful. We're so lucky to have this place. One day, if you make it, you can have a place like this of your own. Isn't it like a spa?"

Um, sorta?

I walked in and introduced myself to his fiancée. She seemed nice, well put together. Then I took my first good look at my new agent: curly red hair, short, stocky. He had mastered that whole studied-disheveled look that goes over so well in L.A.

He definitely had a bit of ye olde Napoleon complex in him, too—he had a lot of bravado and a profound need for everyone in the world to find him irresistible. (Note to agents: If you're reading this book, you should know that you are actually resistible. And everyone can tell you have issues with your height. Your facial hair and scented candles do not distract us.)

It didn't take long for me to realize that it wasn't the girl he wanted me to meet; it was the dogs. He had asked me if I could house-sit, but never mentioned the dogs. Clever move! Let me just say, I like dogs as much as the next person—as long as the next person is someone who only likes dogs a little bit, but not that much.

But: three bulldogs? These were really big puppies. *Puppies.* They hadn't been trained and had no idea how to calm the fuck down. As far as they were concerned they were the stars of a puppy porno and my leg was Jenna Jameson's pug.

I held my tongue. God forbid I should lose my first agent in less than twenty-four hours.

"Do you like dogs?" he asked.

"Ohmygodareyoukiddingme?! I love dogs."

"Great. This is Ruby, Jack, and Sam. Now, you have to make sure to address Ruby first," he explained in a very intense tone. "She is the alpha dog. She needs to be loved, fed and touched first. And . . . you are the alpha human. Did you know that? You're the human."

Um, yeah. Go on.

"And you need to make sure they know you're the human. So, what I want you to do is—wait, are those clothes expensive? Doesn't matter. I need you to lie down on top of the dogs and establish dominance."

Wait, no, don't go on.

"Uuuumm . . . actually, I think I'll try this little technique another time, if that's okay?"

I was still hoping not to fuck it up and insult my first agent.

He agreed that it made more sense for me to "establish dominance" later when he wasn't around. Because his presence would take away my leadership in the wolf pack. As they saw him as their paternal leader.

Okay, got it, dude.

We toured the house. I noticed the coffee-table books: *Raising a Champion*, and *Dog Owner's Guide* and *How To Tell If Your Dog is Psychic*. There were *Vanity Fair* magazines piled everywhere. *Ev-er-y-where*. The bathroom

smelled like a candle had thrown up. There were, like, no less than fifteen candles going at once, all with a different scent. The computer room was locked and I was not allowed in. And then there was the bedroom. He really wanted to show me this one piece of art. Not including the dogs, of course, it was the one thing he'd grab in a fire.

I stared at it, trying to take it in. To make some sense of it. The picture was a collage of black and white photographs. It was hard to make out what it was. My new agent stood

"My girlfriend's vagina. In every position you can think of. Isn't it beautiful?"

just to the right of me, proudly watching me diagnose his masterpiece. I couldn't puzzle it out, so I moved up close and put my face within inches of the piece. And then it hit me.

"Is that . . ." I started.

"My girlfriend's vagina. In every position you can think of. Isn't it beautiful?"

To me, vaginas look like messy open-faced Reuben sandwiches . . . not mine, of course. But, this one looked like that. And so . . . this was his girlfriend's vagina? The woman in the kitchen who was right now establishing dominance over the dogs? I was staring at her hairy snatch right then?

My mind, ever helpful, kicked in with an insta-mantra: *Don't lose your agent. Don't lose your agent. Don't lose your agent.*

"Wow . . . it's really . . . amazing. I've never seen a vagina up close before . . . and wow. Great work."

That was the last day I house-sat for him. And the entire time he was my agent, I never booked a job. Never did establish that dominance, either.

Lesson to be learned? You may be a desperate newbie and really, really, really want to make it. But if someone ever offers to be your agent, it's not worth straddling his dogs and admiring his girlfriend's hairy vadge.

58008

chapter three

the sweetest moments in geek history! of all time!

1391 B.C.: Moses commands—He led the Hebrew slaves out of Egypt, crossed the Red Sea, and delivered the Ten Commandments from the top of Mount Horeb, all while looking like a tenure-track math professor.

575 B.C.: Pythagoras theorizes—The first man to call himself a "philosopher." He also founded a religion based on math and was deathly afraid of legumes.

December 14, 1503: Nostradamus born—apothecary, seer, original know it all.

17th century: Bow ties are donned—First dressed the necks of Croatian mercenaries. Later appropriated by crafty conservative television pundits to look more smarter.

July 10, 1856: Nikola Tesla arrives—Invented radio and alternating current. He also kept a pigeon as a pet about which he said, "I love that pigeon as a man loves a woman." He died alone in New York.

February 5, 1943: Nolan Bushnell changes geekdom forever—Bushnell is born on this day and in 1972 creates Atari. Pixels will never be the same.

1954–55: J. R. R. Tolkien writes geek mythology—Annoyed by England's lack of native mythology Tolkien creates *The Lord of the Rings*. In the process he also invented Orcs. And dorks.

October 28, 1955: Bill Gates hatches—The first person to make being a geek seem a little bit evil.

July 4, 1961: Richard Garriott falls to Earth—He made his first video game as a teenager. Used his gaming fortune to fund a trip aboard a Russian Soyuz, where he made the first sci-fi movie filmed in space. Shortly after, he officiated the first wedding held in zero G. All hail The Pope of Geeks.

May 13, 1964: Stephen Colbert born—Possibly speaks both Quenya and Sindarin.

1966: The Society for Creative Anachronism begins—Cosplay for old people.

1972: Hacky Sack is invented in the state of Oregon, of course— Geek stoners discovered pot and then a little knitted ball with beads in it. Not normally procrastinators, nerds while away precious hours they could've spent on early computers.

May 25, 1977: Luke Skywalker says, "But I was going into Toshi Station to pick up some power converters."

May 14, 1984: Mark Zuckerberg is born—The twenty-five-year-old college dropout's wealth fell half a billion dollars in 2009 to just under a billion. Goes to show, stay in school, kids.

July 20, 1984: Revenge of the Nerds hits theaters—Nerds get revenge.

August 2, 1985: Weird Science premieres—All computers should make hot women. Every single one.

November 24, 1988: Mystery Science Theater 3000 premieres—Heckling science fiction B-movies with wise-ass cracks—once only the province of late-night geeks in their dens—given public voice by a man and his robot puppets.

May 10, 1994: Weezer debuts—With songs about Buddy Holly, sweaters and girlfriends, and a video featuring the band playing Hacky Sack. Lyrics include: "I've got the Dungeon Master's guide; I've got a twelve-sided die."

February 5, 1999: Rushmore is released—Max Fischer: The greatest geek protagonist in cinema history? He did save Latin, after all.

2000: A man named Miles Rohan founds The Corduroy Appreciation Club—The rest of the world gets wise to what geeks have known forever—corduroy rules. And it feels really good on the upper thigh.

December 2003: Battlestar Galactica (re-imagined)—A TV show for nerds that's as good as *The Wire.* So say we all.

November 22, 2005: Achievement Whores keep . . . whoring—Such people will one day understand the true meaning of the word "achievement," set down the controller, step outside and discover what the rest of us call "sunlight."

June 29, 2007: iPhone touches down—It makes fingertips even more useful, has a built-in vibrator and access to the Internet. The best sex toy that can also sometimes make a call ever invented.

January 20, 2009: Barack Obama is inaugurated as the forty-fourth President of the United States of America—The nerdiest country in the world, finally gets the egghead president it deserves. God bless this great and geeky nation of ours!

chapter four
star wars can totally help you in life

It probably won't shock

you to learn that I like the original *Star Wars* quite a bit. I'd probably say I like it as much as the next guy or girl. Well, not if the next guy is the kind who dances around his apartment to DJ Chris's "Fette's Vett" while wearing only his banana-hammock and a Wookie mask. But you know what I mean. The film is an iconic pop-culture creation and touches a bazillion filmgoers to their very core.

It can also be very useful. Useful? What the hell am I talking about? Glad you asked. What I mean is the way that George Lucas's masterpiece contains lessons that can and should be applied to real life. The one that jumps out at me is the message of The Force and how if you stay pure and good and mentally sharp you can, in fact, conquer the Dark Side.

For me, the Dark Side is all the people who have tried to hold me back or undermine me or have stood in the way of my dreams. (Sorry, just lapsed into my own personal *Behind the Music* episode.) When that happens, I metaphorically lift my hand up and use Jedi powers to restrict their breathing and then pick up a drinking glass and smash it in their face. Okay, yes, it was Darth Vader who likes to restrict breathing and he *is* part of the Dark Side, so this metaphor is faulty—but

Yoda is too much of a pussy to restrict breathing.

I can't help it if Yoda is too much of a pussy to restrict breathing and then smash a glass in someone's face. Seriously—Yoda, sweetie, baby, love ya, but you're not exactly considered a badass.

Here's a quick story illustrating what I'm talking about. I studied journalism in college, and one of my first jobs after

graduating was on the assignment desk of a local TV affili-
ate in Tulsa, Oklahoma. That is quite possibly the worst job
in all of journalism. You have to sit there listening to a million
(yes, one million) police scanners going great guns all at
once and pay attention to catch something—anything—
newsworthy on the scanner, like a four-car pileup or a bank
heist. I never really cared that much and so I was never that
good at it. But it was a job, and it was fine. So, end of story,
right? Not quite. See, there was a group of people there
who were mean to me—like, vicious. I found out once that
some of them were e-mailing each other about cutting my
brake lines and carving letters into my skin. Sick shit, you
know? I took to working twenty-hour-days on Saturday
and Sunday so I wouldn't have to come in during the week
and deal with them.

I worked there for a year, because I promised my mom
I would give it an honest try. As soon as that year was up, I
bolted. And as soon as I gave notice, wouldn't you know:
all the psychopathic haters were suddenly so nice to me
and wanted desperately to know where I was going. I
smiled, gave them nothing and didn't let their negative
creepiness slow me down. And never looked back. I just
got all Jedi on their asses and was like: "Who is more fool-
ish, the fool or the fool who follows him?" Ya know? Wait,
does that make sense in this context? I think so. Wait.
Read it back . . . Yeah, it totally does.

*   *   *

In any case, let me just say that even if I am not a *Star Wars* obsessive who camps out for weeks to be first in line for the next installment (not that there's anything wrong with not having anywhere to go to the bathroom), I absolutely appreciate the great film's place not only in geek canon, but in the real world. Lessons can be learned from each and every movie in the series. Like take this lasting and most important lesson from *Return of the Jedi*: If you ever have the option, always, always wear a gold bikini. Trust me, I know, I've done it once or twice.

chapter five
random true story #1

I had this boyfriend

once and after we had sex one night we were lying in bed watching TV and cuddling. Suddenly he turned to me and confessed he wanted to tell me something about himself that he'd never told anyone. I was excited—girls love sharing and learning about the man they're with. I perked up and cuddled closer to hear the mysteries of the guy I had become so fond of. Was it about how he hopes to have kids someday? His dream job? How hot he thinks Alyssa Milano is and I remind him of her?

And then he said it:

"Sometimes I fantasize about sucking a dick."

My eyes became as big as saucers. I answered with a surprisingly simple question: "Sucking your dick, or someone else's?"

He responded: "No one's dick. It's just a big, black dick and it's just sort of floating out there. And I suck it."

Me: "Do you *want* to suck a dick?"

Him: ". . . . . . . I don't know."

There was a long silence. Then I asked, "Do you want me to find you a guy so you can suck *his* dick?"

He sat there for another long stretch of silence.

Then he said, "No. But, thank you."

We broke up the next day.

He was a nice guy.

I hope he finally got to suck a dick.

chapter six

sex: what you can do to help yourelf have more of it

INTRO: As that great

twentieth-century thinker, George Michael, once so eloquently put it: Sex is natural and sex is good. True. But may I be so bold as to add: Sex, great sex, can be very hard to have. But, yes, it is natural and good and with a few pointers, you too could make it GREAT. So that is why I would like to now offer a few ideas for how to make it less weird, even more fun, and occur way more often. Unlike most sexual encounters, I don't think you'll be disappointed by my advice.

1. Wrap it Up, We'll Take it

You always dribble before you shoot, so make sure to wrap it up. Translation: Do not have sex without a condom. Even if you plan on pulling out, a few drops of your man-juice can spill out before you do and then, just like magic, it's kid time! Sure they can be cute, but it's so not worth it. Yes, guys will say that you can't feel anything with a condom, or they want to raw-dog it be-

You always dribble before you shoot, so make sure to wrap it up.

cause it makes them feel closer to their girlfriend. But let me reiterate: No matter how good the sex is, even if she is Giselle Body-By-God Bundchen, it's not good enough to pay child support (roughly 30 percent of your income) for eighteen years. So wrap it up! Also, if you get an STD, you're marked for life. Herpes, genital warts, AIDS (AIDS!), hepatitis—that shit's for life. Sex, on the other hand, is just for two minutes!

2. Listen to Your Lover (Or Babe, Sweetie Cakes, Hot Rod, Honey, Dancing Queen, Dairy Queen, etc.)

If she tells you she likes it when you bite her neck—do it! It doesn't matter where she learned that she likes it or why she does, just be thankful you got the tip. Girls don't always express what they want, so when she does say it, you really want to make sure you are paying attention. Also, learn her language (unless it is Mandarin, because that shit is impossible). If you start pulling her hair and she starts moaning, that's her way of saying, "*Ohmygod,* please do this more, and by more I mean all the time." And the more you please her, the more she'll want to do it with you. It's a win-win!

3. Get Down and Dirty

Okay, I know a lot of people have a hard time talking dirty—they don't know what to say, how to start, or when to end it. Also, at first they will think they sound ridiculous. And they might. But let me just say that talking dirty is so important in sex. And it's pretty easy. To wit: establish from the very beginning that you like this. And trust me, you want to do it early on. Because if you wait too long to introduce the concept, your Special Lady Friend will be a little thrown and might not take you seriously. Think of it as a hat. If you never, ever wear a hat and one day you try to rock a fedora with a feather, all of your friends will be like, "Dude—why are you wearing a fucking fedora with a fucking feather?" You'll feel insecure and never wear it again. Now imagine that scenario, but in bed with your hardened dick out and it's your girlfriend saying, "Dude—why the fuck are you talking like that?" Not good.

So, how do you start? I think a simple text message from the beginning of the relationship is perfect. Send a text that says, "Hey, I wish I was inside you right now." (Ed.

Note: Do not send texts like this if you are thinking of running for public office, *or* text only from one of those Go-Mobile pay-as-you-go phones.) It's specific enough and kinda dirty, but not degrading. She'll get excited that you're thinking of her and so turned on with the text that she'll engage in your sex-text conversation.

Now here's the best way to talk dirty. Forget everything you've seen in porn (and, yeah, everyone knows about your porn habit)—that doesn't work for girls. It's simple. Just describe what you want to do to her. Whatever you do, just be very descriptive. When you're taking her clothes off, tell her that you've been thinking about being inside her all day. Describe how it feels for you, how you want it to feel for her. Then pray to God it hasn't happened in your pants already so she can rip them off you.

4. The Art of Seduction

Lord knows it ain't easy keeping the love alive, but there are ways to do it that don't involve *Cosmo* magazine or duct tape. First off, always switch it up. That doesn't mean you have to dress like a perverted pirate and drop down from the ceiling. It just has to feel fresh. Like the moment she opens the door, grab her, shut the door and have your way with her right there in the foyer. Just that little moment will keep things exciting.

Or make a pact that you won't have sex for a week.

(What? A week is a long time!) The buildup will be so intense that you will both, inevitably, break the pact, but the sex will be amazing and you'll feel closer, having broken the rules together.

And this is a tad more ambitious, but totally worth the effort: If you are driving by yourself and see a place that looks great for fucking—a clearing in the woods, a roadside waterbed, etc.—remember it, then drive back by with her in the car. Pretend like you just thought of it and tell her you want to have sex in that open house . . . but only if you can afford the mortgage because there's a good chance she won't want to leave! In which case, don't forget to have your mail forwarded and the cable disconnected back at the old pad.

chapter seven

my fans rule—
and are really good artists, too

San Diego's Comic-Con

International is my favorite convention to go to all year. It's like the mothership calling me home. It's filled with fans dressed up as their favorite characters, movie stars, smaller specialty stars and exclusive set pieces flown or shipped in just for the convention.

It really is the one place where you can set free your inner nerd without any shame. You can dress up as Jar Jar Binks and fall in love with someone else dressed as Silk Spectre . . . and no one judges you. In fact, everyone embraces it. Yes, even Jar Jar!

Nerd. Geek. Used to be if you self-identified that way, you'd get thrown into a locker and never have sex. Or worse, whatever that is (have you seen the size of those lockers???). But to me and more and more people I know, being a nerd or a geek means having passion, power, intelligence. Being a nerd just means there is something in the world that you care deeply about—be it twelve-sided dice, a favorite sports team, your new laptop or *Knight Rider.* And I've always found geeks sexy. If you look back on all the guys I've dated (with the exception of a few douches here and there) most of them are dorky-looking. But what I've always found attractive about these kinds of guys is their ability to be passionate about something (usually video games and *Star Wars*, in my experience) and not be ashamed of it. It's really sexy to be around someone who knows how to tear apart a computer and put it back together—and loves doing it. Maybe I'm alone in this, but I don't think so. Nerds are sexy.

And Comic-Con is nerd heaven. I love spending time with them, mingling and meeting—hell, I am one myself. One year at Comic-Con security threatened to shut down G4's live show because so many fans had gathered near our stage and they wanted to avoid a fire hazard. But, I really wanted to spend time with the fans who just wanted a picture or an autograph. So, after the show, I spent five hours signing every magazine, picture, and T-shirt that the fans wanted ink on.

I don't get people who don't get why I like spending time with the fans. I mean, why wouldn't I enjoy that? One of the most important things to me in my work is the fans. I know that without their support, I wouldn't have any of this. It might sound cheesy but it is so true.

Oh, and another great thing about nerds? Their artistic abilities and witty senses of humor. Seriously. My fans are really funny, clever and sarcastic. And often times they show it with their fan art—artistic tributes to my spazzy, superfun and, yes, nerdy existence. I've been lucky enough to accumulate a nice collection to share with you. So please enjoy a few examples of these marvelous creations.

Fork That!, by Laura Babcock | Rarely, if ever, have we seen such a perfect rendering of om nom nom.

Devil Girl, by Isaac Richardson III │ A throroughly meta examination
of what it means to be human in the 21st century in super hot jeans.

Excuse Me!, by Andy "Savory" Wilson | An exquisite study in realism.

Freckles, by Chris Nelson | Haunting use of negative space.

Munnyuns, by Kris Ayres | This is a poingant comment on hyper commercialism and of, oh fuck it … Funions! Yum!

Munn Hope, by Josh Wilson | An interesting statement on presidential campaign art. And Wonder Woman.

Snack Time, by CRXTHRASHER | Mmmmmm, pie.

Unwound, by Emil Agarunov | An interesting statement on outmoded technologies. And hot cleavage.

Red Hot Pooper, by Andre Walker | Excellently captures the subject in her natural habitat.

Still Life with Top Hat and Giant Bunny, by Jeremy Natividad │ A surrealist masterpiece. Plus: bunnies are cute.

Liv Pen, #2, by Diego Nunez Castellanos | Exquisite employment of crosshatching.

Cosmo Munn, by Ben Precup | This vision of a paranoid, techno-future thrums with the anxiety of a world in which machines rule us and well-crafted underwire bras are essential to one's survival.

TOP RIGHT: **Ownage**, by Jeff Kim | A dynamic exploration of the real. Also: don't fuck with me.

ABOVE: **Floaterbot**, by Mark van Olmen | Vividly captures the isolation of a modern existence and how, in the future, we will take our joysticks everywhere, even into the stomachs of our personal robot slaves.

Zombie Munn, by Doug Circle ¦ Reminiscent of classical baroque-period paintings, if classsical baroque-period paintings featured more zombies and mysterious dead girls bobbing in pools of blood.

PiePhone, by Kris Ayres | Finally, an app we really want.

chapter eight

the first rule of kindergarten is that you have to bribe kids to let them play with you

When I was two

my mom married her second husband. He had two kids and one of them was Annie, a girl around the same age as me. She was beautiful. She had long blond hair, light eyes and was very girly and sweet. I was the polar opposite: polyester pants, striped boy long-john shirts and long, tangled, black hair. Not girly at all.

At four we went into kindergarten together. I remember she wore her favorite yellow dress with ruffly bloomers underneath and hair in two perfect pigtails. She was so excited for school and friends and learning. Then there was me—blue polyester pants, red striped sweater, hair pulled into a ponytail because it was too tangled to do anything else. The only thing we had in common, it seemed, was that I was equally excited about meeting new friends. And skin—we both had skin over our bones. So there were two things we had in common.

On the first day of school Mom drops us off at the door of the classroom and turns to leave. Annie and I walk into the class and follow the teacher's instructions to hang our backpacks on the hooks and pick a seat at a table. I hurried over and threw my backpack somewhere and went to find a seat and maybe a new best friend! I head for one seat and almost reach it when the girl sitting next to me puts her hand on it and says, "This isn't for you." I turned and looked for the next open seat. There were just two left. One was at a table full of girls and the other was a table full of boys. Like most girls at this age, I hated all boys except for my brothers.

One of the girls at the all-girl table motioned for me to come sit with them. I smiled, relieved I dodged the alternative, and grabbed the seat. Before I could sit down, the girl looks at me confused and says, "No not you . . . *her.*" Annie was walking up behind me and took the seat at the table . . . and I went to sit with the boys. *This isn't for you—* those words still make me want to throw up and cry and develop a prescription drug habit that I know won't really help me in the long run but will bring sweet, sweet relief in the moment.

As the months went on in this class, I watched Annie make lots of friends and every teacher dote on her. Annie was always great at being loveable and pretty and smart. And I could see how much adults loved it. They loved it so much it made me not want to be like that at all. Why couldn't adults be nice to me simply because I was a little girl who tried to do the right thing? Just because I didn't always wear perfect dresses with the perfect matching bow didn't mean that I wasn't a sweet girl, too.

From very early on in my life I realized how most people are nicer to prettier people. I know that sounds horrible, but think about it. Look around. Look at how you act with attractive people. It's like a moth to a flame. A gorgeous, beguiling, astonishingly attractive flame. Little Annie with her sweetness oozing out of her pretty pigtails was hard not to love. And little Olivia with her freckles and mismatched leggings was a little easier to overlook. I don't think it means we're bad people for catering to the perfect . . . I honestly don't think it's a conscious decision. But when you've been on the other side of it, the side that is pushed out of sight, you become very aware.

In this kindergarten class, there was a playhouse in the back corner. And because it was a small enclosed area, the teacher had a rule that only five kids were allowed to play house at a time. And to keep it fair, it was the five who got to the house first who could play in it. Playing "house" was my favorite game. I loved acting out different parts of the family and play-cooking and -cleaning. So every playtime I would race to the back corner and jump in the house. "We've got one!" I would yell. And the other girls would race to the house. And every day, there'd be one too many girls who wanted to play. And every day the other five girls, including Annie, would turn to me and say, "We don't have room for you and we want to play." So, with what little pride I had at four years old, I would hold my head high and act as if I didn't really want to play. "Oh, I know. I didn't want to play house. I was just holding it for you guys." Could you just die?!

It crushed my heart every single day. I didn't understand it. I was always nice to everyone. I swear. I ended up realizing through life, that at that age, kids looked at Annie and me as two sisters to choose from. One or the other. And for whatever reason, I never got to be the one they wanted.

It crushed my heart every single day. I didn't understand it. I was always nice to everyone. I swear.

I remember once Annie coming home with a birthday invitation from one of the girls in class. She handed it to my mom and asked if she could go buy a present for the birthday girl. My mom turned to me and asked if I wanted to go pick out a present, too. I told her that I actually hadn't been invited. I remember the look on my mom's face. Pure anger. She picked up the phone and called the girl's mother and asked her how she could invite one sister, but not the other. That phone call earned me my own invitation to the party. But I didn't want it. I knew it was a pity invite. And I would much rather be at home playing LEGOs with my brother than be with some girl who didn't want me there. Yes, I was hurt. And yes it was embarrassing to see my mother so confused with the fact that I wasn't invited. I was less confused. I knew that I just didn't fit in.

Then, one day after I was kicked out of the playhouse yet again, I came up with a plan. A genius plan. You see, there was no baby doll in the playhouse. *Every* playhouse needs a baby doll. So that night, I took all the books and papers out of my backpack and stuffed my Cabbage Patch doll into it.

The next day playtime was called and I got up and ran to the house, just like I did every day. I was hoping I wouldn't have to resort to Plan B. I was hoping that maybe this day would be different. Maybe this was the day they wanted to play house with me, or at the very least be short one person and could let me stay. I stood at the front of the house, hopeful, and counted five girls walking up.

It was time for Plan B.

I went over to the hooks and grabbed my backpack and pulled out my doll. I was sitting directly in their line of sight. And then I unfolded my brilliant plan. I began playing with my baby doll by myself, making big, oversized gestures and rocking her and laughing and cooing loudly so they could hear. Out of the corner of my eye I could see them stop playing and notice me . . . they were whispering . . . it was working! I continued to play as if I didn't see them at all. Then one of the girls walked out of the house and came over to me.

"Hi. Can we use your baby doll? We don't have one." Aha—she walked right into my baby-doll trap!

"Yeah, you can use it," I responded, playing it cool. "You can use it if I can play with you guys."

She looked at me, looked at the doll and turned back to the house. She started whispering to the other girls, then turned back around toward me.

"Okay. You can play with us," she said. "But you have to be the dog."

The dog?!! Seriously. The dog? Hells, yeaaahh!!!! I was gonna be the dog! I know now how pathetic and sad that was. But in that moment, I felt happy. I was playing house with them and that's all I wanted. Bring on the dog!

Oh, and one last thing: You know about the rule, right? Oh, yeah, I didn't know this back then, but apparently it's a steadfast rule: When you play house, the dog has to stay outside.

chapter nine

my dinner with
harvard's finest

One night I was at

dinner at Ago with a friend, a famous Hollywood director and the famous Hollywood director's girl-friend *du jour*. We were sitting there eating a massive spread of carpaccio, caprese, steaks, and pastas, and drinking what I'm assuming was really, really expensive wine (I really don't know wine at all—in fact, I think Boone's Farm is delicious). As we sat there, the waitresses, restaurant managers and chefs all came out to kiss the ass of the director sitting to my right. No one seemed to mind the fact that he was throwing food into his mouth like a baby whale, and there was an interesting green stain down the front of his shirt, even though there was nothing *green* on the table. I guess the rest of us weren't entertaining the director enough so he took it upon himself to do the entertaining.

He turned to his date—a very thin, beachy-blond-haired, twenty-three-year-old, wearing tight jeans, a T-shirt deliberately ripped to hang off one shoulder and red-soled Christian Louboutin shoes—and he says:

"Doesn't she look like a whore?"

Just like that. Like he was asking if we thought it might rain later. The three of us sat and stared, waiting for him to continue his train of thought because it was clear this was a rhetorical question. Also, I suppose there was some morbid curiosity—I for one was wondering if this train of thought might smash into the mountain of asshole-ness. Excitement!

"She went to Harvard, but she looks like a fucking whore."

Okay, here we go. I couldn't stop staring. She was sitting directly in front of me and could obviously hear every single word. It looked like that had affected her but I wasn't totally sure. I didn't bother looking at Director Guy, as I'm sure he was just staring at her as well, waiting to see how far he could go.

He continued, "I mean, people who go to Harvard are smart, right? She's not. She's just a whore. Look at her. She just looks like a slut."

Boy, I wonder how he talks to people he *doesn't* like. Or maybe he didn't like her? He just wanted to fuck her? Los Angeles was still a strange new world for me, and I didn't yet understand the often insane-seeming ways its denizens interacted. The weird part: He said all this with a smile and a laugh. Kind of the way

"I mean, people who go to Harvard are smart, right? She's not. She's just a whore. Look at her. She just looks like a slut."

girlfriends will talk with each other—you know, "Shut up, you whore!" But this was different. There were no giggles, no trust built from years

of friendship and bonding. Just . . . eww. Right?

The girl sat there for a moment, then summoned her grand retort: "Shut up."

She didn't say it with authority or with fear or really any emotion at all. You've got to feel it, sister! Shut. The. Fuck. Up. Followed up with a cocktail shower! That's what she should've done. But she didn't.

So he continued, "Why did you go to Harvard if you're such a slut?"

I have to confess I was intrigued. (Does that make me a horrible person? Don't answer that!) Most women would be appalled to hear a man degrade another woman like that. And I am definitely one of those kinds of women. Generally I find this kind of boorish, sexist behavior as nauseating as mom jeans. But all of it was complicated by the fact that she had made a specific choice to hang out with this guy . . . this director . . . this slobby boy who's famous in

Hollywood not so much for his body of work, but for his ability to be such a complete and utter asshole. So this was more entertaining. I mean, why should I or anyone feel bad for this girl, who clearly chose with her own free will to hang out with this douchebag just because he's famous? I was intrigued at this interaction. And I soon found myself asking:

"Why are you putting up with this?"

Instant silence. Everyone turned and looked at me, including the director. It felt odd to put the girlfriend on the spot like that, but shit, what was she thinking? Her response did nothing to illuminate that.

"Putting up with what?"

Dude.

"Um, putting up with him calling you a slut and whore and trying to embarrass you in front of us "

She sat there collecting all of her Harvard thoughts and then after a deep breath said something that you could tell she thought was poignant and profound and made complete sense. "Okay, like ninety-nine percent of the time he's this asshole. But, one percent of the time, he's really, *really* amazing."

She seemed very content and proud of her answer. The director, beaming, looked back at me for my response. He was obviously really enjoying this.

I said, "Okay, see that busboy over there? What if he

was one hundred percent of the time as amazing as you say ass-scratcher here is one percent of the time—would you hang out with the busboy?"

The director knew exactly where I was headed and quickly turned and asked with a very large and amused smile, "Yeah . . . why are you hanging out with me?"

She thought for what seemed like five minutes as we all waited, the director with a huge smile on his face, so happy with the conversation. Then homegirl finally took a deep breath and, to no one in particular, said:

"Shut up."

I couldn't help myself—and yes, this was maybe not my proudest moment—and asked, "Have you fucked him?"

This time she was quick to respond, "No! Of course not . . . I've only sucked his dick."

What? I swear, I couldn't make this shit up. And she said it with a straight face, without a hint of embarrassment.

The director, meanwhile, wouldn't let the answer to the previous question slide and asked again, "So, *would* you hang out with the busboy?"

She took another long breath and then stood up and said, "Shut up. I went to Harvard and I don't have to take this."

All right, there it was. Finally. I felt good—she had stood up for herself (literally!) and I'd helped her do it. Amen!

Look, the fact of the matter is that she was a pretty girl who came out to Hollywood for fame and fortune. She somehow met this director who had all this money, power and fame, and she got lost for a minute. Maybe she thought that some of his good luck would rub off on her. Who knows? But now she had finally stood up for herself. She realized she doesn't need him, his connections or his money. Hallelujah! She was saved!

Or was she?

Girlfriend grabbed her purse, then turned around to face the director. She was going to tell him off. She was going to tell him not to call her a slut or a whore, to really let him have it. She was not going to let him get away with treating her like that no matter who he was. She took one last deep breath and said:

"Give me some money. I have to pay for valet."

Are you kidding me, woman?!

He reached into his pocket, pulled out a roll of hundred-dollar bills and handed her one. She looked down at him, threw down the bill and grabbed the entire roll from his hand.

I guess you really *can* buy love—or whatever passes for it in a dimly lit banquette at Ago.

I sat waiting for my car while she drove hers away from valet. And that's when I saw it: a bumper sticker on her Toyota Forerunner announcing to the world: UNIVERSITY OF NEW YORK COMMUNITY COLLEGE.

So. Awesome.

chapter ten

the rewards and pains of designing your own presidential campaign platform

1. I will designate $3 billion in taxpayers' money to the invention of affordable hoverboards.

2. I will fix America's obesity problems by taking all motorized transport away from fat people. In turn, I will build an infrastructure of Fat Tunnels, where all the fat people can walk. This will create jobs and subsequent weight loss.

3. The judicial system will be abolished in favor of a UFC/MMA fight between the two opposing parties.

4. The creation of a new cabinet post, Secretary of Bread and Gardening. Guess who the first appointment will be? My mom!

5. Pie would be its own category, placed at the top of the Food Pyramid.

6. Change the official language of the United States. The new language: texting.

7. Everyone is now required to adopt one Asian baby. Even Asians.

8. There would be a permanent ban on balloon-popping. Not balloons, just popping them. We will just have to wait and watch them get saggy, sad, and eventually be no fun for anyone. Yay?!

9. Forget what I said about pie as a category. Pie should actually be our new monetary unit. People will now haggle by saying, "That's not worth 5 Meringues! Maybe two peach cobblers *at most*."

10. Every citizen will be required to take an Asian-Recognition Course. This will enable everyone to appropriately identify what kind of "–nese" an Asian person is. This should drastically reduce the number of people who think I am Japanese.

chapter eleven

what to do when the robots invade
(yes, when!)

Sometimes I like to

joke about the fact that pretty soon the planet Earth will be invaded by a robot army that will quickly overtake the U.S. military, the UN and even China to conquer the world and make us their slaves, just like in a science fiction story. When that happens we will all toil in a gray-black *Blade Runner* universe until we die at a tragically young age, cold and alone, on the futuristic chain gang. It's hilarious, see? And also not that farfetched—I mean, we already have robots working in some of this country's most powerful sectors like politics (where they've served as White House press secretaries for the last three decades), business/retail, and media. But perhaps I should stop joking and get serious because it seems that this possibility is entirely too real. And, um, what then? Let's explore.

As far back as the year 2007 CBS News reported that scientists at Tokyo University had built a robot nurse that "follows you around with all your pills and potions, and tells you off in a hectoring tone if you forget to take them on time." I know what you are thinking: How do they know those are robot nurses and not just someone's mom? Good question. The answer: they just do.

As if that isn't sinister enough, the Koreans are apparently working on a robot soldier that can move, detect an assault, shoot in retaliation, play poker for cigs and jerk off to porn. Okay, not really—everyone knows robots don't smoke! And right here in the good old U.S. of A., the Pentagon would like to soon launch what has been described as an "airborne robot hit man," which sounds like *Iron Man*, but with none of those messy human emotions and feelings.

So what does all this mean to you and me? Probably nothing. But maybe everything. Feel better? No, really, I'm no alarmist so I wouldn't be saying all this unless there was something to it. I think the best thing we can all do for now is be vigilant, but not too vigilant. Like, I don't think you need to go out immediately and buy a shitload of survivalist gear—night-vision goggles, a flashlight, bottled water, a new sleeping bag, microwave popcorn and a gun that can kill robots—but in life it is always best to be prepared. That means there are a few basic precautions that we can all take should this fantastical notion actually happen in real life. Below, the three best plans for combating a robot invasion, in order of effectiveness.

- **Learn how to deflect an attack from a robot's laser eyes.** This is not as hard as it sounds. All you really need is a metal trash-can lid, a lightweight thermal shirt that breathes and a small, cute kitten. Here's what you do: When it becomes apparent that the robot in front of you plans to attack with laser eyes (this will be evident because the eyes will turn red, which is the color of lasers), grab the kitten and throw it in the *opposite* direction of where you intend to run. The robot will be distracted and may even zap the poor little creature to lifeless fluff. That's sad, but when the robot invasion comes, you will think that is much less sad than it seems now, trust me. With its attention shifted to the airborne kitten, you will only have a few seconds to make your break, so don't dawdle—no Facebook

> **All you really need is a metal trash-can lid, a lightweight thermal shirt that breathes and a small, cute kitten.**

status updates, no G-chatting, and especially, no tweets! Just run. You will likely escape but if the robot still manages to zap at you, raise your trash-can lid (which has been strapped to the forearm connected to your non-driving hand by a *super* strong twine), to fend off the attack. With any luck you can redirect the laser beam to cause a dii)ct hit on the robot's heart—or what passes for a heart in that tin chest of his, strangled with wires—but any kind of redirection will work. Once you have successfully executed that maneuver, continue running. You will actually run a lot while escaping the robot's laser eyes, which is why you are wearing a thermal shirt that breathes. That's called thinking ahead!

• **Make the robots fall in love with you.** This is admittedly trickier to pull off than the above idea. First of all, how do you know if it is a male or female robot that is attacking you? Well, you might not, but that doesn't mean this technique still can't work. Everyone craves love and affection, after all, even robots. And it is possible that all robots, as they are from the future, are bisexual, so don't let figuring out its sex distract you from the urgent matter at hand. What my research has indicated is that, when it comes to being crushed on, robots are very much like human women: they like conversation, someone who is a good listener, a frequent bather and, more often than you might think, movies featuring Kate Hudson. And gifts. And reverse cowgirl, which they call—get this—"reverse robot-girl." If you can successfully get the robot to fall in love with you, that will greatly reduce the chance that it will mangle you with its insanely violent metal claw-hands or singe you with those aforementioned laser eyes. Romance has never been more complicated—but the payoff here (getting to live) is huge.

• **Hide really good.** Just because robots have laser eyes doesn't mean they have *X-ray vision*, right? So it's a good bet that you can actually simply hide from robots in a well-constructed fallout shelter in your backyard, at a Detroit Lions football game or while mingling at the Cheney family reunion (and you just know that Lynn cooks up a mean-ass BBQ!). Of course this approach still requires sacrifices on your behalf. For instance, your life as you know it will never be the same and you can never see your family again. So there's that. But isn't that a small price to pay for the very sake of our great nation? Because if we don't give up our lives in order to go to the awkward family get-togethers of former vice presidents and then hork down on free BBQ, then the robots have already won.

To be clear—and because my legal team made me put this part in—none of these ideas are guaranteed to save your life when a robot army invades our land. (Yes, *when*.) But what they will do is this: allow you to trick yourself into thinking you have a chance. While spending more time with cute kittens and the Cheneys.

chapter twelve

I've never been into

stimulants. I've never smoked weed or done mushrooms or Ecstasy or any drug that wasn't prescribed by a doctor. Never even smoked a cigarette. I drink from time to time, but not that much. Not because I'm a saint or conservative or think there's anything wrong with doing recreational drugs (as long as you don't hurt anyone). I just have never had any desire to do them. And also, aside from it never smelling or looking good, I don't like the way I feel when I'm drunk and not in total control of myself. Because when I'm not in control, something like this next story is inevitably going to happen.

* * *

A couple of years ago I was at a destination wedding in Mexico and I had about six or seven tequila shots. I had just recently learned how to properly drink tequila shots. The trick is to never taste it. To begin with, you have to drink Patrón Silver because it's the cleanest and doesn't have that thick tequila taste. And after every shot, you chase it with pineapple juice. The juice is so acidic and strong, it instantly kills the taste of tequila. And that's why someone like me, who never drinks, can do six or seven shots in one sitting. (You're welcome for that tip, by the way. Just be careful!) Tequila is great as long as you don't know you are drinking tequila.

At some point later in the night, sometime after my seven shots, so hard to know exactly when, the bride grabs my hand and takes me up to her hotel suite. She reaches into her bag and hands me a little white pill.

"Here, take this," she says, as she downs hers. "It's a Soma. Muscle relaxer."

I'm already wasted, of course, and so I think that a Soma sounds like a great idea. Within minutes we decide we need to get everyone, including the mother of the groom, in the ocean naked. Obviously. Naked Wedding Ocean Party!!!!

We run downstairs and corral the whole wedding party out to the beach. It's Mexico, so the water was as warm as a bath—no excuse not to go in. I watched as everyone stripped down to nothing. Now, by the grace of God, I somehow did not get naked. I remember thinking that if I did, my then-boyfriend would be so angry with me. Especially since there were men around that I didn't know. So I ran into the ocean fully dressed.

A Fun Fact about muscle relaxers? They relax *the hell* out of your muscles. Yeah. I guess when you're drunk and taking pills from a bride's purse, you don't really think about what that means. Now apparently it can be very dangerous to take a muscle relaxer. People have been known to break bones while using a relaxer because their muscles can't support them or something. So think about that. Now think about me, seven shots of tequila in my body *and* I'm on a muscle relaxer *and* I'm swimming in an ocean at night. Fully dressed. So I start to do what anyone in those circumstances would do: I start to drown.

I'm flailing around, not able to control my arms or legs and laughing hysterically with every gulp of ocean water I accidentally swallow. Thankfully my boyfriend is watching all this unfold and he jumps into the ocean to save me. I remember hearing him scream my name and seeing him come for me. And then I remember thinking we had started a game of "Marco, Polo" and so I begin swimming away from him, deeper into the ocean. I get to a point where I am literally beginning to drown. I can't stay afloat. Just then I feel an arm come around me to pull me back to shore. When we get back to the beach, I'm gasping for air and lying in the sand. We're both coughing up ocean water. As my boy-friend lies there in shock over how close I was to drowning, I bounce up and follow the maid of honor, who screams for me to come take a shower. You heard that right. The maid of honor screams for me to take a shower. With her. (Note: You are about to be fully rewarded for buying this book.)

I leave my boyfriend on the beach, pretty oblivious to how stupid I was being and how I put both of our lives at risk, and run up the stairs to the nearest room. I strip down and the maid of honor and I jump into the shower and warm up under the single showerhead. Now, I don't know who initiated what or how it started, but next thing I know, I'm kissing her in the shower . . . with the water falling on top of us. I know! I had never, ever, ever kissed a girl or even come close to that. This was my first brush with a lesbian experience ever. Need a minute? Okay, I'll continue.

We're in the shower kissing and making out. At one point I put my hands on her chest to feel her breasts. She was a gorgeous girl with a great body, but she was really flat-chested. Which actually might have worked out in my favor. I started to feel her up and thought to myself as I touched her breasts, "Oh . . . she's like a boy." Not in a bad way at all, because remember she was a gorgeous girl. Just that she had very small breasts. And since I'm not a lesbian (and I'm pretty sure she isn't either) in that moment it was kind of comforting to find something familiar in this very not-familiar situation.

I'm sorry to have to tell you that my first lesbian foray ended quickly after we knocked over a champagne bottle that was sitting on a shelf in the shower, brought in, I'm assuming, for Olivia's First Gay Night of Fun. After it shattered all over the shower floor, we had to leave. How we were able to do that without cutting our feet wide open? I can only guess that it was the power of same-sex love that carried me over the broken shards of glass.

The last thing I remember is pulling out shorts and a T-shirt for her to wear and saying good night. I don't remember falling asleep or changing into pajamas or anything. My boyfriend said he came in the room right after our shower (oh too slow, sorry!) and helped me into bed. But for some reason, and maybe it was just a dream, I remember things a little differently. But since I'll never know for sure, let me leave it for you all to decide.

What do you think happened after I made out with the maid of honor, broke a champagne bottle and gave her some dry clothes to wear?

I:

- ⓐ Fell asleep
- ⓑ Went to her room to finish what we started
- ⓒ Had an orgy with her husband and my boyfriend
- ⓓ Went back to the ocean and almost drowned again

Maybe one day I'll tell everyone what I think really happened. Maybe I'll put it in the next book. To be continued. . . .

chapter thirteen

surefire pickup lines for college kids trying to nail their teachers

How many of you

have had a crush on a teacher? I mean, remember that Physics professor? Law One is so steamy, I'm getting worked up just thinking about it: Every object in a state of uniform motion tends to remain in that state of motion unless an external force is applied to it. *Mee-yow.* Okay . . . maybe that was just something I experienced.

But just in case you've gone through the same infatuation I have, I've come up with a list of lines you can use on your, um, object of desire— whether they instruct in history, math, English or a foreign language like the language of love! Memorize these can't-miss lines and you'll be on the dean's list for doing it in no time.

1. I'm interested in speaking with you about opportunities for extra credit.

2. Need anyone to clap your erasers?

3. My dog ate my homework— while I was busy eating Ecstasy.

4. Rush week is every week at my personal sorority of one!

5. Here's a flyer for the Roman Polanski Film Festival I'm putting together.

6. Wait—you're a fan of the Dewey Decimal System, <u>too</u>?!

7. Nice tie.

8. Nice shirt.

9. Nice lecture.

10. Come here <u>often</u>?

chapter fourteen
a gallery of great women

Some women achieve

remarkable greatness by soulfully stitching together the rough red, white and blue fabric that made up the very first American flag, thus bringing Old Glory herself into existence. Other women find greatness in the hot chamber of a .22-caliber rifle. Others marry into greatness and then play an integral part in the fight for civil rights for every human being on Earth. And some women assume the mantel of Empress of Russia before allegedly assuming the position in order to make great, sweet love to horses. Some simply rock their great asses in electric blue short shorts adorned with glittering stars.

So while all of the great women portrayed here in this Gallery of Great Women arrived at greatness by vastly different routes, they all helped pave the path before me. As a woman, I am always looking to other women for inspiration, courage and determination to help me achieve in what is still, in many ways, a man's world. Several of the women pictured here have inspired me in just that way, and I am not only talking about Wonder Woman, Princess Leia and Sailor Moon. The others are pretty cool, too. Please enjoy these stirring and heroic images of great women throughout history.

Betsy Ross, 1777

Annie Oakley, 1881

Wonder Twin, Jayna, 1995

Catherine the Great, 1761

Princess Leia, 1977

Eleanor Roosevelt, 1933

Wonder Woman, 1941

Sailor Moon, 1993

Pocahontas, 1615

chapter fifteen
on the *playboy* cover shoot, scandinavian stylists, and picking out panties

Something totally crazy

just happened to me and I have to tell you about it: I got the offer. Yep. The cover of *Playboy.* I was really surprised. I thought the only people who were offered a *Playboy* cover were celebrities trying to prove they're still hot at forty, and reality stars with sex tapes. Let me check—nope, I'm neither of those things. I had done a celebrity page for the magazine a few years ago, but that wasn't anywhere near nude or as high profile as the *cover.*

My publicist and I instantly—and politely—responded with, "No, thank you." But, still, I couldn't resist telling everyone that I got the offer! It was hilarious to me. I mean, I'm not super-skinny, I don't have huge boobs—and do people really know who I am? I was flattered. To be offered the cover of *Playboy* is prestigious in its way . . . or was at a time. And I was pretty happy to get the offer—even if I did turn it down. Without even asking how much it would've paid. From what I hear, to do a nude cover could've easily fetched a cool seven figures. Seven! As in the number just after six! Wow . . .

So why didn't I do it? Well, first off, a million dollars is not enough for me to get nude for the sake of . . . getting nude. Second, everyone I knew agreed with me that it was not the right time. When is the right time? When I want to prove I'm hot at forty! Thirdly, I couldn't imagine my stepfather, brother, or cousins seeing me spread-eagle in any magazine, let alone spread-eagle surrounded by feathers or pearls or on top of a car or eating a cheeseburger or whatever the hell else it is people do while they happen to be butt-ass naked. But more than all of that, I couldn't and wouldn't do it because I didn't want the fans to be disappointed.

Okay, maybe that sounds crazy. I know a lot of people think my fans are sweaty, overweight geeks who *want* to see me naked. Well, they might be right. But they're mostly wrong. I think the fans would look at me like a sellout, a fame whore who is trying to get by on her looks alone—well, that *and* her vagina. My fans and I have something special that most people in the spotlight don't have: it might sound cheesy, but the truth is we are friends. And I wasn't about to let down my friends.

So I turned down *Playboy* and everyone I knew was in support of it. Oh, wait. Everyone except for one of the higher-ups at G4 (the network I host *Attack of the Show!* on). I sent the Playboy e-mail to a bunch of my colleagues as a "can you believe the offer I just got?" laugh. I was surprised by the response; people thought I should do it—saying it would be great for my career. In some ways, I think they were right. Everyone would know my name for like a week. Sure, my "career" would be "great" for a week. What about after that? I'd just be another chick who got naked for *Playboy*. And at this point, there isn't a price tag on that for me.

A few weeks later I get an e-mail from my publicist. It's *Playboy*. And they're offering me the cover . . . again. But this time *no nudity*. Wait. What? They want to put me on the *cover* of *Playboy* and I *don't* have to get naked? Weird but true. *Playboy*, it seems, is in a rebranding period and they thought I represented the "new era" of Hollywood, celebrity and all that stuff. Wow. Okay. I'm in.

For this shoot, I requested my normal glam team—makeup artist, hair stylist and wardrobe stylist. *Playboy* sent some suggestions for photographers they wanted to use. I chose a photographer I'd previously worked with on a different magazine shoot and whose work I really like.

I get a call saying that this photographer insists on using a different wardrobe stylist. He has a guy that is "fantastic" and "would really make the shoot great." Some photographers in this business insist on working with the same stylists, makeup and hair people. So much so that sometimes the entire shoot hinges on it. Now the same goes for the celebrity. Especially for someone like me. Look it—I'm half Chinese and half white. My face is not like a normal person's—my cheeks are big, my eyes are small; a little bit of makeup goes a long way on me. And despite my hair being heavy and long, it can hold a curl super well. These are all things you have to know to help me look my best. I've had one too many bad experiences with so-called "fantastic" artists and stylists and I didn't want the cover of *Playboy* to be something I wasn't proud of. Like that time I made out with that boy throughout the entirety of *Forrest Gump*! (See page 138.) This was not about to be another *Forrest Gump* make-out session!

But this photographer was really pushing his stylist on me and since he had done numerous *GQ UK* covers and we could talk about the look and feel of the shoot ahead of time, I figured it would be okay.

I had once seen some pictures of Heidi Klum that I liked. She was sitting on the grass, smiling and being very flirty, playful and summery. I sent the pictures to the photographer, stylist and *Playboy*. Everyone loved them and agreed the shoot should have the same spirit.

Playboy then said that if I flash the same amount of skin that Heidi had, they would pay me a certain amount—I'm not gonna reveal too much here (it's a trend!) but suffice it to say it was a very good amount of money. No seven figures, of course, but still. Heidi had only showed some side boob and maybe the top of her butt. Hell, I'd shown that much in surf magazines. We agreed. After all, I wanted the pictures to be sexy and would've felt comfortable showing that much with or without the money.

Yes, you can show underboob, but there can be no areola. Again, only side boob, no pink anywhere.

Before the shoot, my poor publicist had to have legal conversations that I'm sure she'd love to forget: side boob, no nipple, no pink. No butt crack, but you can show top of back. No vagina, no anything. Yes, you can show underboob, but there can be no areola. Again, only side boob, no pink anywhere.

By this point, I'd had numerous conversations and e-mails with both the photographer and the stylist. Everyone was on board and it was gonna be a great shoot.

The day before the shoot I go and get spray-tanned at *Playboy*'s request—they want me to have a nice glow. I like a good glow as much as the next girl, so sounds good to me! The night before the shoot I eat a salad of iceberg lettuce, tomatoes and balsamic vinegar for dinner and hit the hay at 10 P.M., wanting to get all the beauty sleep I can.

I wake up the next morning at 6 A.M. and head to the shoot at a house in Venice. When I get there my makeup artist is setting up and the stylist, Gustav, whom I had only spoken to on the phone, was lining up shoes. He is a tall, heavyset, bald man from Scandinavia with a very heavy accent.

"Oh my God! Gorge! Gorge! So much more gorge! Olivia, you are so gorge! You have to see this stuff I get for you. It is so amazing . . . Zia is ze one that Steven ze photographer just loooooooves."

Suddenly and quite horrifyingly, he pulls out—and I'm not making this up, I swear—a black, fishnet, one-piece bathing suit where you can see *everything* going on. And by everything I mean my vagina would be completely exposed and look like a honey-baked ham trapped in supermarket netting. Um—no! On the top were two small, pink half-cups. As I scanned the teeny tiny garment—waiting for the punch line to this bad joke—Gustav explained:

"You would be wearing nothing under here and then your boobs just hang right over ze pink part. Zis is sooo gorge, no?"

Before answering I scanned the rest of the clothes on the rack—black leather, shiny silver, crazy tranny heels. Wait, is that a whip? Holy crap. This is nothing like we discussed. Fun, flirty, playful? What the hell?!!

I calmly tried to gather all the spit in my very dry mouth that I could and said: "Um, this is a non-nude shoot. I told you that."

"Vat? Oh, no dahling. Zis is *Playboy*—you show *every-thing!*" Gustav replied.

"No. Who told you that? I told you it's not nude. We talked about this. There's a contract that says no nudity." I felt woozy and tried to understand what the hell was happening. When had I wandered into a Franz Kafka story as imagined by Larry Flynt? Was I about to turn into a giant insect wearing a leather G-string?

"Steven—ze photographer. He says all nude today for Playboy. It's *Playboy!*" Gustav responded again in a very what's-wrong-with-you attitude.

I told him to go get the photographer and I got on the phone with my publicist and told her to get there right away.

When Steven arrived he had the same opinion and then added, unhelpfully, "Oh, yeah, you'll be nude but we'll just Photoshop everything out."

Luckily my publicist got there right then and let them know there would be no nudity and that there was a contract to confirm it. That seemed to be the end of that conversation.

As the shoot goes on, my publicist and Gustav bicker nonstop. She doesn't want a lot of jewelry, he of course does. He thinks I should show more skin, she of course doesn't. The photographer isn't doing much to help ease the tension. He wants me to pose nude, while strategically placing my arms and legs; my publicist of course doesn't. He wants to do a shower scene nude with strategically placed bubbles and steam on the glass; my publicist of course doesn't. It's exhausting. All the while I'm trying to pose flirty, fun, summery with about five dudes—strangers working the set—watching my every move. One of the shots has me without a top and my long, thick hair covering my breasts. The whole time I'm worried about the wind blowing, exposing a nipple, the filthy five and the photographer snapping away because that's the shot he wants.

I can hear them bickering again with my publicist. The photographer and stylist insist they've shot more revealing stuff for *Esquire* and *GQ*.

Of course you have! I think to myself. Afraid to speak up and yell at everyone because it would ruin the shoot. I'm the one who sets the tone and energy on the shoot. If I show everyone I'm upset, the shoot will spiral downward faster than it already has. What I want to say is this: "Of course you've shot more nudity in those magazines! It's not *Playboy*. *Playboy* still has a stigma. I've shown more of myself in *Vanity Fair*. But that's different. If I show more in *GQ* I'm being artsy and sexy. If I show more in *Playboy*, I'm just one more tart in . . . *Playboy*."

Getting the cover, and not having to be nude, was a huge deal to me and my team. Only a handful of people have done it without having to take it all off. And here we are, contracts decided, conversations spanning weeks about this day, and everyone has a different agenda.

The bickering escalates right before my cover shot. We've done about four looks already, all the while my anxiety is skyrocketing from the tension and my feelings of not trusting the stylist. We are in the dressing room with my makeup artist, publicist, Gustav the stylist and his two assistants. He wants me to—surprise, surprise—wear a see-through top and nothing underneath. My publicist says . . . well, I bet you can guess what she said. Then I see something I thought I'd only see in a Christopher Guest mockumentary—the chubby, tall, bald Scandinavian begins to scream at my publicist inches away from her face and not much farther away from me.

"You know what?! I am a great stylist. I am not one of ze . . . ze Hollywood stylists. I am European!! And this is not all about Olivia, okay? It iz about me, too! I have my own motivations with this shoot and I'm going to get what I want out of it! Zis iz *Playboy!!!* She haz to be naked! If not, why iz she do *Playboy*?"

Now I can't take it anymore. All the excitement and preparation leading up to this day had been gone since before I took my first shot. I really couldn't deal with it anymore. My publicist was doing a great job standing up for me, but I thought I was going to have an anxiety attack if I didn't say something.

"Look, Gustav, *Playboy* came to us and asked me to do a nude cover. We declined the offer and then they came back and offered us the cover, no nudity. We have a contract that says this and you and I have discussed this as well."

My publicist chimes in, "Yes, Gustav. The big deal about this shoot is that she *doesn't* have to *get naked* and she *still* gets the cover. They came to us. We didn't go to them."

Gustav, now looking like a very big, juicy—but not so much delicious—Scandinavian tomato, gets closer to my publicist's face and says, "Fine! You zink you are so good at style? You pick out ze panties!"

He flips his head back as if he had a mane of hair atop it, puffs out his chest and as he reaches the door, he snaps his fingers and says, "Girls, let's go!" And as if they are tiny toy poodles, the two assistants who were arranging shoes on the ground, leap up and scurry out behind him, their four-inch heels clicking all the way.

The door shut and we all sat in stunned silence. I was fine dressing myself, but I didn't know where anything was. I was sick to my stomach and wanted to leave. But it was an expensive shoot and I knew I had to keep things copacetic if we were going to finish the day. I called the photographer in, told him what happened and he went and spoke to Gustav.

Moments later he came in as if nothing was wrong, no apology, just came back in. He wasn't helpful. He just said yes to whatever we asked. But we didn't want a yes-man. We wanted a stylist who could offer his expertise and input, but could also stay within the concept and contract of the shoot.

We go upstairs to the rooftop pool to get the cover shot. As soon as we get to the top, clouds blacken the sky and the wind blows the pillows off the chaise longue chairs. It was like the last scene of a slasher film. If I didn't know better I would've guessed this was God telling me to run . . . Run as fast as I could.

And as if the energy wasn't already bad enough, it just got worse. Everyone is freaking out.

"You can't replicate the sun in Photoshop!"

"The wind is going to make her hair look so messy!"

"She'll be too cold and you can't take away goose bumps easily!"

"The wind is rippling the water—it doesn't look as beautiful and still and wonderful as the rest of the shoot!"

After about an hour of awesome awkward silence waiting for the sun to come out, I jump into the pool. I've managed to bury my feelings deep, deep inside—just the way Dad taught me! Yay! And everyone seems to have moved past the horrible confrontations and bickering and negative energy . . . or maybe they've just learned to bury it deep inside just like me.

We're in the freezing pool shooting for hours. That was the only way to keep warm—so I did it. Good Lord, did I do it. I peed like I had never peed before and I'd been drinking Big Gulps every hour on the hour for the better part of two decades. The water was suddenly significantly warmer and . . . urinier?

Finally—mercifully—the day was done.

I was mentally and physically exhausted. I kept smiling but really I wanted to break down crying. I felt comfortable and sexy in front of the camera and thought the pictures reflected that . . . but, man, it wasn't easy.

On my way home, after not eating much of anything for about two weeks leading up to the shoot, I stopped by a Mexican restaurant for its "Taste of Mexico" menu. I sure wanted to taste some Mexico. The menu included: one tamale, one enchilada, a beef taco, beans, rice and guacamole. The taste of Mexico! The taste of freedom! I downed it all with a Diet Dr Pepper and crashed out by 8:30 P.M. I slept a full twelve hours that night, with the makeup still on my face.

I woke up happy that the day was behind me and I had done my best.

Then I checked my e-mail. Ugh—the photographer said he didn't think we had the cover shot and wanted to try again the following week. *Playboy* and my publicist agreed. I absolutely insisted on my own stylist, agreed on a date to shoot and mentally prepared myself to not eat any sweet, sweet pie for yet another week.

Sometimes, especially on misty fall mornings, I find my mind wandering, thinking about what Gustav is up to at that exact moment. What does Gustav look like while eating breakfast? Orange juice pulp speckled on his lip, his nuts scrunched into mesh underwear. Maybe he's a sad and frustrated artist, trapped in his work as a stylist to surly stars and stars in waiting (hello!). Van Gogh with a B-movie bad-guy accent. Then I start feeling guilty. Maybe I should call Gustav, see how he's doing, say wut up. But then the image of that black, fishnet bathing suit pops into my head and I think—no, no I shan't be calling Gustav any time soon.

And that's okay. We can't, after all, be best friends with everyone we meet, right? The truth is, Gustav isn't a bad guy—we just had different visions. He thought I would look great with my female junk squeezed to resemble overripe fruit in a leather G-string. I did not. *C'est la guerre.* Nine times out of ten these shoots go amazingly well and super smooth. Every once in a while, though, the stars are not aligned (unaligned?). At times like those, it's important to remain a pro, to get the job done, pass the ball, shoot the fish, dunk the goalkeeper, and carry the torch without starting some wild-ass conflagration. You know? At times like those, just refrain from kneeing anyone in the nuts. Because then everyone wins! And instead of using ice on everyone's nuts we can put it into a blender and make a smoothie or a rum daiquiri!

chapter sixteen
the time i met the champ

When I was twenty

years old, I came out to Los Angeles for a meeting and an audition. I came alone because it was just for a few days and I didn't think I needed anyone with me. I wasn't old enough to rent a car, so I had to take a taxi to the hotel in Santa Monica. Once I got to the hotel, I realized I had nowhere to go. Without a car, I was stuck. And then it hit me—the biggest ball of anxiety I'd ever felt. I started to think about my situation. I came all the way out to California by myself for an audition. What if I bombed? What if no one liked me? It was horrible. I was all alone and crying in this very sad Santa Monica hotel, worlds away from any comfort.

I picked up my cell and called my sister. She told me to just get out of the hotel. Get in a cab and go to a mall. At least there would be other people around and I could distract myself from my worries and anxiety with shopping. When I got to the Third Street Promenade mall, I just started walking around. And she was right—I instantly felt better. As my tears dried up, I walked past a Foot Locker and a tall black man exited the store. I continued walking until I heard behind me: "What's your name?"

I turned around and said, "Olivia." The very tall guy I just passed put his hand out to say hello and told me his name: "Hi, I'm Evander Holyfield."

"Yeah . . ." I responded. "I know."

He asked where I was going and I told him I was on my way to grab lunch at this Italian restaurant. He asked if he and his assistant could join me.

A few minutes later we were sitting in this empty Italian restaurant, Evander Holyfield on my left, his assistant to my right. Just an hour ago, I was sitting in my dark hotel room crying, feeling sad and lonely, and now I'm here with the former heavyweight champion of the world.

The waitress took my order: meat lasagna and a house salad. Evander looked at me and said, "Is your mom fat?"

"What?" I responded.

"Is your mom fat? Does she have a big ass, big thighs?" he asked.

"No. She's not fat," I answered.

"Good. Then you can eat the lasagna. If your mom's not fat, you're not gonna be fat. But if you're mom's fat—you can't eat that lasagna," Evander explained.

"Good. Then you can eat the lasagna. If your mom's not fat, you're not gonna be fat."

Lunch was pretty quiet. He asked me where I was from and other simple questions. And then toward the end of my fatty fatterson lasagna, he asked me one last, simple question:

"I got eight babies, by eight different women. You wanna have my ninth?"

I sat stunned, not so much by the question itself but at how easily and matter-of-factly he had asked it. "No thank you," I said.

Before we finished lunch, I remembered to look. The ear! How could I be this close to the man and not look at the infamous ear that Mike Tyson had once nibbled upon as if it were meat lasagna and he had a fat mother? So I did. And for those of you who ever wanted to know: yes. Yes, there is a scar on his ear and yes, it looks like someone took a big-ass bite out of it. Now that I think about it, I'm glad I didn't look at the ear before ordering lunch.

chapter seventeen

... help you score!

Dating—apart from

trying to figure out why the hell some starlet's boobs hang so low, is there a bigger mystery in the universe? I say no, but I also say there are a few easy ways to take a little bit of the mystery out of it. I know it sounds crazy, but it's true. And take it from me, I should know: I've had, like, five whole boyfriends in my life and only one of them had Tourette's and another one was the maybe-gay son of a famous general . . . . Anyway, read on to learn how you, too, can conquer the confusion of courting.

1. Pack up that Pickup Line

Girls know if they like a guy from pretty much the first moment they see him. Ipso facto (Latin, bitches!): No pickup line will work. Even if you come up with the wittiest, funniest, most brilliant I-can't-believe-you-just-said-that-please-allow-me-to-rip-off-all-my-clothes-right-now line, it won't matter if she's not physically attracted to you. "Hello, I'm Jeff" is the best pickup line you can have. Especially if your name is Jeff. Ditch all others.

2. Slow Down, Speed Racer

Okay, you've negotiated the dangerous, shark-infested pickup waters and met a girl who's awesome and you decide she might be the one—or at least the one for that night and she could possibly even get you to change your Facebook status. What to do then? Buy her something sparkly that you totally can't afford from Tiffany's, right? Because nothing says I love you like going into massive debt! Wrong. Wait at least six months before splurging for that extravagant gift. You want her to feel special, of course, but buying her pricey items right away might make her feel like you are upping the seriousness factor too soon. Relax. Play it cool for a while. Have her over to your place for a *Guitar Hero* night or to watch *The Dark Knight*—and make sure to fast forward to all the Joker scenes; they're really the best. Practice your Dirty Sanchez or Donkey Punch or Strawberry Lemonade (Urban Dictionary, please). Because if the whole thing goes up in flames after two months, I guarantee that you won't get the diamond tennis bracelet back.

3. You Don't Have to Pay to Play, um, Player

It's sooooo annoying when girls think that guys should have to pay for everything. That mentality is ridiculous and ancient. Any female who's worth having around, will offer to pay her portion—and maybe even the whole bill. I always offer to pay for my share, and often the entire tab. Part of the reason I want to pay is to tear down the idea a lot of people have about women expecting men to pay. I wouldn't call myself a feminist, but still. That's backward and bullshit and I think any self-respecting chick will say the same thing. So even if you fully intend to pay for the meal, make sure she at least makes a move for her purse. If your special lady friend doesn't even attempt the time-tested Fake Purse Reach (FPR), drop her. She's not worth it. Who wants to be with someone who thinks you should pay for everything? And if she's having you fork out for fish 'n' chips, just imagine what she will expect you to pay for down the road. Now, all this being said, it's still nice when the guy refuses to let you pay. So another tip here: as the meal is winding down, slip away to the bathroom and hand off your credit card to the waitress. When the bill comes, it'll be taken care of and you'll look like a P-I-M-P. That spells Pimp for all you illiterate or blind people out there. Hey, if you are blind or illiterate, how are you even reading this?! Sneaky robot eyes you must have!! Speak like Yoda, I sometimes do!

4. Signature Moves are for Suckers, John Hancock

You might want to get comfortable—this one takes some

'splaining. Once you have a live, naked girl in your bed, don't fall back on boudoir tactics you've had success with in the past. I honestly don't know why more people don't complain about this phenomenon. Sure, sure, I get the appeal: If it's not broken, don't fix it, right? Fine, but pretty sure that idea doesn't apply to sex. Vaginas are, after all, like snowflakes, only warmer and softer, and bleed like a gaping wound monthly . . . wait, what was I saying? Oh, right, vaginas are like snowflakes in that each one is different. So that fancy two-finger swirl trick that worked wonders on your last

Once you have a live, naked girl in your bed, don't fall back on boudoir tactics you've had success with in the past.

girlfriend? Yeah, no guarantee it'll work the same way on the new one.

Another risk: if your signature move is too specific, it could backfire. How? She'll know instantly it's your "move," dude, and that you are very likely thinking about the last girl you pulled your "move" on and how "enflamed with passion" it made her. And you never want to put the ex back into sex—you dig?

The first time I realized all guys have signature moves was when I on my very first date. I was fourteen years old and his name was David and his last name started with an "R." So naturaly he insisted that everyone call him "D.R." or simply "the Doctor"! I'd like to give you a description of what he looked like—so you can see exactly what's burned into my memory forever. (We can suffer together!) The Doctor was Filipino, only a couple of inches taller than me, with tall spiky Asian-styled hair (read: created out of borderline illegal amounts of L.A. Looks gel). He favored oversized jeans, carefully penned-upon blue Converse sneakers, and a really large No Fear T-shirt that announced to the world: A TRUE WARRIOR NEVER FIGHTS WITHOUT A PURPOSE THAT IS GREATER THAN ONESELF. Okay, buddy, whatever. We decided to go to the movies, but we lived on an air base in Japan, so we didn't have the choice of what to see. The theater always played hits that had been released years earlier in the U.S. Now, I'm not sure how this happened, but I had gotten it into my head that when you go to the movies on a date, you have to kiss *the entire time*. Ironically, I must have learned that at the movies: I mean, in every freakin' flick, the couples are making out. How could I know any differently? Ask my mom? Uh, no. Here's that scene:

Me: "Hey, Mom. So I'm going out with the Doctor . . ."

Mom: "Who? What his name?!! What his parent do?"

Me: "Ummm, I don't know what his parents do. His name is David R.—you know, the Doctor."

Mom: "What?? The Doctor? That stupid name. You tell him you no go out tonight."

So, not an option. Anyway, I went into this movie date with the idea that you have to make out the whole time, no exceptions. And I have to say I was excited about this idea. Up until then, I'd never really thought about kissing boys. And if I did, it was only when I practiced on my cold wall. Yeah, I know. It was weird. I don't know why I didn't just practice on a stuffed animal, a Ken doll, or my hand like normal girls. Weird.

So we're sitting in the dark theater and as soon as the first scene begins, I turn toward his seat and go for it. Like a desperate, horny virgin in a porno called *Desperate Horny Virgins*, starring me. We start making out . . . and we don't stop . . . for the entire movie. Did I mention we'd gone to *Forrest Gump*? Yep. We made out through *Forrest* f'ing *Gump*. The whole thing. One hundred and forty two minutes of lip-twisting ferocity. His tongue was practically slathering my tonsils through young Forrest's awkward childhood. His hands were down my shirt and cupping my boobs (actually my very padded training bra, to be exact) by the time Forrest was learning all about every type of shrimp in the world. You remember: boiled shrimp, grilled shrimp, barbecue shrimp . . . French-kissing shrimp. My lips went numb during the Vietnam War and by the time Forrest came home to possibly get an STD from that whore Jenny, the Doctor did something I wasn't quite sure about. His signature move.

Let's see—how to describe this? Okay . . . ummm. He stuck his thumb into my mouth. His whole thumb. Like a giant, bendy thumb-shrimp! He was staring straight ahead

at the movie, trying to pretend that this was the most normal thing in the world. After two small circles around my
lips, he just shoved his entire thumb into my mouth! Then
he starts to swirl it around . . . in my mouth. His thumb was
in my mouth! I didn't know what to do, so I just sat there.
He started to move it in and out of my mouth, as if I was
giving his thumb a blow job. I suspected he'd done this a
few times before, and that was confirmed when he turned
to me and whispered, "You like that, right? I know it feels
good."

Forrest was about to marry Jenny and take care of their
bastard son, but I didn't care. I just wanted Nogi's damn
thumb out of my mouth! The moral of the story? Just because the last girl liked sucking on your thumb, doesn't
mean I will. In fact, I know that historically I have not en-
joyed it at all.

So in conclusion: Signature moves suck worse than
having a thumb shoved in your mouth. Or anywhere else,
for that matter.

chapter eighteen

my worst day ever

You know that feeling

when you just want to be left alone? When you just want to shut your bedroom door on the world for a day? Well, I went through that, but instead of it being just a day, it was about an entire-year phase.

I graduated high school and moved in with my grandparents, who lived just blocks from the college I was going to attend. I was going through some intense teen angst.

"No, Grandma, I don't want any food."

"No, Grandpa, I don't want to go to church."

"No, Grandma, I don't want to watch *Wheel of Fortune* with you guys."

"No, Grandma, I'm still not hungry."

They were the sweetest people in the world. But, to me, they were just annoying. I knew at the time I was being a brat, I just couldn't stop it. Or at least I didn't stop it. I really wanted to just go to school and then come home, without being offered eight things to eat, to go into my room and crawl under my blanket and not come out until the morning.

It was a really depressing time. I didn't have any friends, mostly because I didn't join a sorority. And my biological father had moved back in with his parents, my grandparents—just two bedrooms down from me. Totally uncomfortable since I never had a great relationship with him in the first place.

One day my grandma insisted she take me shopping to find a new comforter set for my bed. She thought something bright and cheery would help lighten my mood. At the time my room was disgusting. There was literally trash piled all over the floor. I remember seeing an apple core stick out of a pile of papers in the corner of my room. I agreed with her that I needed a change and went along as she picked out a canary yellow, flowered comforter. And you know what? For a time, it kinda worked. I felt happier. I opened my shades and let the sun hit the swirly yellow and pink flowers.

But, eventually, the depression came back. And there was a good six months of just anger where I was being a complete bitch. I honestly couldn't stop it. I hated running into my dad in the house, talking to my grandparents about school, being told to turn the TV down in my room . . . everything was agonizing to me.

And then my car broke down. Looking back, I feel it was a blessing from God. It was August in Oklahoma—insanely hot and humid and hot. My car breaking down meant that I wasn't going to walk to classes. So, while my car was in the shop getting fixed, my grandparents drove me back and forth for four days. Normally, at this time of my so-called life, I wouldn't spend that much time with them, but relying on them for transportation forced some quality time on me.

One afternoon Grandma picked me up from class, and since we had a few hours before the next class, we decided to grab lunch at a local burger shop. As we sat there eating our burgers and crinkled fries, I kept thinking to myself, *Just say it. Say it now . . . Just say it.* So I did. I looked at my grandma, took a breath and said, "I'm sorry. I'm sorry I'm such a brat. And I'm sorry I get mad so much. I don't know why I'm like this. I'm sorry if I ever hurt your feelings. I don't mean it."

Without missing a beat, Grandma simply replied, "I know. You don't have to be sorry. You're just going through a tough time, that's all."

I felt such a relief. I may not have been able to stop being bratty and bitchy and wanting to be left alone, no matter how bad I wanted to, but at least I managed to say I was sorry. I meant it.

The day after our lunch out, Grandma and I waited in the covered patio while Grandpa pulled the minivan out of the garage. It was extremely hot that day, even more sweltering than usual. I could feel droplets of sweat trickling down my back. Suddenly my grandma, who had been standing right next to me, stumbled. She took a step back and caught herself on the patio wall. I asked if she was okay. She insisted she was and went back inside to get some iced tea to cool herself down.

Later that day as I walked through the kitchen on my way to my room, another bout of bitchiness came over me. I just wanted to be left alone—again. My grandmother was wrapping a wedding gift for my uncle and his new wife. She stopped me to ask how to spell his wife's name. Of course, this annoyed the crap out of me for no good rea-

A. Me as a baby. I was a really chubby baby and everyone always carried me around, so I didn't even walk until I was two because I didn't have to. (Courtesy of Olivia's Mom)

B. You can see in this picture, especially with the blue jumper on, how much I looked like a boy. Everyone thought I was a boy. I have so much hair now it's hard to believe I had that little amount of hair until I was two—basically bald. It used to drive my grandpa so crazy he taped a bow onto my head so people would stop saying "what a cute little fellow." (Courtesy of Olivia's Mom)

C. I'm the baby being awkwardly held by my cousin Jonathan . . . hhmm . . . now, that I think about it, that's probably why I hate redheads to this day. I kid, I kid! (Courtesy of Olivia's Mom)

D. This is one of my favorite pictures. It's my sister, Sara, and I. I remember taking this picture and being so happy to wear my Rainbow Bright dress. My grandma took us to get this picture taken and let me pick out my outfit. Usually, my mom demanded what I would wear in all pictures. So, this was very exciting for me. (Courtesy of Olivia Munn)

E. For some odd reason, every year my parents put a sheet up and had all the kids dress up and take pictures in front of it. I think it was our version of a Sears portrait. (Courtesy of Olivia's Mom)

A. My grandma and grandpa would always drive us from Oklahoma to Las Vegas to see my biological father during the summers. And we always made a stop at the Grand Canyon. I look bored because this was probably my fifth time seeing one of the "Seven Natural Wonders of the World" as I was often reminded by Grandpa. (Courtesy of Olivia's Mom)

B. I went skydiving in Oklahoma when I was 20 years old. That's me safely hitting the ground. I took a four-hour course and they let me jump out of the plane by myself! I remember being so afraid to jump out of the plane and then, once the drop was over and I was floating down calmly, I got really bored. I felt so guilty for not remaining excited. But, honestly, after the rush, it wasn't that awesome. (Courtesy of Cara McConnell)

C. Because of work, I wasn't able to get home for three months after my niece, Ripley, was born. This is the first time I met her. And I've been in love ever since. (Courtesy of Olivia Munn)

D. That's my stepbrother, stepsister, sister, and myself (I'm in front, picture right). We took Taekwondo for almost ten years. We're Asian so that means karate and a musical instrument are nonnegotiable activities we had to participate in. (Courtesy of Olivia's Mom)

E. Little known fact about Tommy Lee Jones? He's a God in Japan. He does these ads for Boss Coffee and his face is on billboards and posters all over Japan. Oh, and Tommy Lee Jones is my dad. Don't believe, check my videos online. (Courtesy of John Boyd)

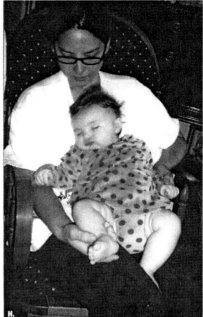

F. For our week of challenges on *Attack of the Show*, my cohost, Kevin Pereira, and I got to fly World War II fighter planes. Seriously. Fly them. Yes, there was someone in the plane with us, but I'm telling you right now, that guy did not touch the controls . . . I wish he would have. Because, yes, I could pose like a badass before I got in that plane, but once I was in the clouds and I've got this German pilot screaming directions at me, I did not feel like such a badass anymore. (Courtesy of Olivia Munn)

G. Yes, I love pie. I love whipped cream, Cool Whip and ANY kind of cream that is whipped. But, I equally love brownies with walnuts topped with whipped cream. I actually don't have a sweet tooth. But these three things are my weakness. (Courtesy of Olivia Munn)

H. My niece, Ripley, is around 8 months old here and at that great age where she's super chubby and cuddly. I used to be baby crazy. I couldn't wait to have kids and would even cross a street just to hold a baby. But once Ripley was born, I stopped being so enthralled with other people's babies, and only wanted to see and hold her. (Courtesy of Olivia's Mom)

I. My niece Ripley just turned 2 years old here. And yes, she's reading a book. She's two and knows how to read. And yes, she'll have to buy my book like everyone else. There are no freebies in this family. (Courtesy of Olivia's Mom)

A. I cohosted two weeks of the *Loveline* radio show with Dr. Drew. It was so much fun and Drew and I get along great. He's hilarious and the two of us together work so well. One time someone called in and told us some horrific thing they did at a sex party called a "chili dog" and by the time he was done explaining what it was, Drew and I were literally out of our seats, jumping up and down laughing and crying so hard. There was about sixty seconds of dead air where we just laughed. (Courtesy of Ann Ingold)

B. Last year in Japan we went to the home of professional sumo wrestlers (everyone from one team lives in the same house). It was a big deal because they don't normally allow outsiders in. They were all so nice and courteous. Even though my producers told me not to bring them Krispy Kreme doughnuts, I did anyways. And guess what! They loved them. (Courtesy of Olivia Munn)

C. This pic was taken right after I jumped off a cliff in Jamaica. If you look closely, you can see the massive bruise developing on my thigh—a result of freaking out moments before I hit the water and turning my legs. (Courtesy Cara McConnell)

D. If you go to Harajuku, Japan, on Sunday, you will see the streets filled with Japanese girls dressed in the most random Cosplay outfits. I went into a store and put on a French maid outfit. But, it barely beat out dressing up as Little Bo Beep. That'll be next year. (Courtesy of Olivia Munn)

E. Part of my show's week of challenges was to get into full special-effects fat suits and participate in a rascal scooter race. An Academy-Award--winning special-effects artist made me up. When we were finally done after hours of makeup he turned me around to the mirror and I started smiling at how amazing the transformation was. He was shocked by my reaction saying that whenever he finishes fat suits on women, they start crying at their reflection. That is so stupid. It's just makeup. Oh, and I won the rascal race. (Courtesy of Olivia Munn)

A. This was my homage to the comedy film *Dodgeball* when I did the cover of *Complex* magazine. Right before this shoot I was doing so much pilates, cutting out all carbs, and doing a lot of praying. I felt like I was in pretty good shape. But, when I went to put on the boots (which were brand new, patent leather) they were hard to zip up because they weren't broken in yet. So, the stylist leans down and starts to try to zip them up and then looks up at me and says "Oh, God. Did you eat those potatoes at lunch?! I don't think these are gonna fit." I responded, "You mean I have fat legs now?" And she said, "Well . . . you just have *strong* calves." (Courtesy of Olivia Munn)

B. I took my brother to Japan with me and we went barhopping in Golden Gai which is an area of town that has tons of tiny five-person bars crammed into one alley. It's what *Blade Runner* was based on. (Courtesy of John Boyd)

C. Olivia's Mom: "Miss Kim" (my mom) with my niece Ripley, who is 8 months old. Both. So cute. (Courtesy of Kim Schmid)

D. William Shatner: I've met him twice, and this was the first time I met him. He was really nice. The second time I met him, he said if I was an escort I'd be "an expensive one." Uhmmm, thank you? (Courtesy of Olivia Munn)

A. Dressed up in Star Trek attire for one of the earlier skits I did at G4. (Courtesy of Olivia Munn)

B. In Japan they have these jelly energy drinks. That was one early morning on a street in Shinjuku and I was sucking down some energy. (Courtesy of John Boyd)

C. This was taken during the 1000th episode of *Attack of the Show*. I absolutely adore my cohost, Kevin Pereira. We were both kind of emotional at the milestone and how we could be part of creating such a unique show that fans actually responded to. (Courtesy of Brandon Hickman) son. I responded sharply, "I don't know. Ask my mom."

I regret that to this day. I wish I could have known what would happen that night. I wish I had acted differently. I wish I wasn't such a spoiled brat. I continued to my room, crawled into bed and turned on the TV. Hours later, I heard my grandma turn off the lights in the kitchen. I heard her familiar shuffling walk down the carpet on the way to her bedroom. I remember thinking to myself, *Please don't stop at my door to talk to me. I just want to be left alone. Please keep walking.*

But she didn't. The shuffling across the carpet stopped right at my door. I held my breath, annoyed. Then I heard her say, "Good night . . ." Her feet didn't begin moving again. She was waiting for my response. I didn't want to respond. I didn't want to talk to anyone. I just wanted to be left alone. So I kept quiet. I couldn't be bothered to say two small words—good night.

At about 3 A.M. I was still up watching TV. I heard a noise. It was an old house, so hearing noises late at night wasn't unusual. But this was different. I muted the television to listen. I could faintly make out my grandfather's voice: "Honey? Honey? Honey, are you okay?"

I got out of bed and walked to their bedroom. I could see the light coming from their bathroom and my grandma's legs sticking out between the doorway's threshold. I turned the corner to see my grandpa holding up my grandma's shoulders as she lay lifeless on the ground, her bare legs extending out of her nightgown. I was in shock. What happened? What's going on? What was I supposed to do?

"Grandpa, should I call 911?" I asked.

"I don't know . . . she just fell," he responded, clearly not thinking straight.

"Grandpa, should I call 911?" I repeated. I have no idea why I didn't just start dialing. Looking back I think I was too stunned. I just wanted everything to be okay. I wanted him to tell me she was fine, it was okay. To call 911 was to admit that something bad had happened. I wasn't ready for that.

I grabbed the phone and called. The operator asked me if she was breathing and what had happened. I didn't know. The only thing I could decipher was a gurgling noise. I told the operator that I could hear my grandma gurgling. The operator instantly said, "Okay, if she's gurgling, I need to give you instruction to perform CPR." But then I second-guessed myself. "No, maybe she's just snoring," I said. The operator responded, "If she's gurgling, you need to do CPR. Is she gurgling or snoring?" Looking back now I know the sound I heard was what people call the "death rattle." The final gasps of air just before you die. I don't know what I was thinking—I was so afraid. I was frozen. I didn't want to give my grandma CPR. What if I hurt her?

What if I didn't do it right and killed her? I convinced myself it was snoring and told the operator CPR wasn't necessary. She told me the ambulance would be there soon.

There was a portable clothes rack next to the doorway of the bathroom. I got up and threw it to the side, bending the metal frame. I didn't want anything to get in the way for the paramedics. When they got there, I wanted them to be able to get right to her.

I went outside to wait for the ambulance. It felt like forever. Literally. I saw the ambulance pull around the corner and I ran to it, jumping and thanking God for sending help. When they finally pulled up to my curb, the two male paramedics moved so slowly. I didn't understand that. This was an emergency. I screamed at them, "Why are you moving so slow?!!! My grandma is in there and she's dying!! You have to go faster! Go faster, go faster, go faster!!!"

They didn't. They continued at their glacial pace. They entered the house and performed CPR immediately. Right then I knew my grandma had died right there. How? Their cat. My grandparents had this really old cat that did nothing but lie around all day long. But at this moment, as my grandma lie on the bathroom floor, the cat started jumping up and down, swatting at some invisible object and meowing into the air. I tried to calm her down, but this cat was way too freaked out.

A few minutes later, the paramedics emerged from the bathroom with my grandma on a stretcher. My grandpa was in a T-shirt and boxers. He followed hurriedly behind them, looking despondent and scared. I ran after them and saw my grandpa get into the ambulance, hovering over my grandma. She had stopped breathing but the paramedics were able to resuscitate her.

I walked back inside the house and called my mother. I told her to make the thirty-minute drive over as soon as possible. I paced, waiting. Then I noticed blood on the carpet. My grandma's blood. Blood that fell in an effort to save her life. I couldn't let my grandpa see this when he got home. I had to clean it up now. I kneeled on the ground and scrubbed and scrubbed until there was no evidence left.

My mom and I arrived at the hospital to good news. Grandma was on monitors and a breathing machine, but the doctor thought she might be okay. I asked to see her, but everyone insisted it would be too traumatizing for me, what with all the tubes and machines. I should just go home, they advised, go to sleep and see her tomorrow when she's feeling better.

I went home and slept well that night, comforted by the thought that I was going to be a different person. I almost lost my grandma and the last thing I'd said to her was, "I don't know. Ask my mom." I wouldn't live like this anymore.

This bratty, bitchy kid. I would appreciate my grandparents and say good night to them. I had to learn the hard way, but I learned. I've been given another chance to do right by them.

I was awakened from my deep sleep by a phone call. It was my sister and she told me to get to the hospital immediately. It wasn't good.

I raced over and sat in a very sterile, white room with my dad, sister, grandpa, our family minister and his wife. The doctor came in and told us that my grandma didn't have enough oxygen to her brain when she collapsed, and she was officially brain-dead. She wasn't going to be okay. We had to take her off of life support.

It seemed so sharp and quick. No one talked about it, discussed other options or asked questions. We sat there in silence. And then as quickly as we were told we had to pull the plug, we were in her room, and the doctor shut off the machine. It was so quick. I could barely even think straight. Where was my mother? She'd want to be here for this. What's going on? Can I hold her hand? Can I ask for a moment to be alone with her before she leaves us forever? Can I just tell her I'm sorry? Can I tell her good night? Please? Please, I just want a second to think.

But, before I could let out a word, she was gone. The machine shut down and she was gone. I couldn't believe it.

I didn't want to believe it. We were all in shock, quietly crying to ourselves. As soon as she died, we left the room.
Looking back, I wish I'd sat with her for a while. But it was
all so sudden and no one knew how to handle it. I was the
last to leave the room. A man came up to me and asked
me for permission to take her body to the funeral home.
Already? You have to take her right now? I ignored him and
began searching for my mom. She was supposed to be
here. Where was she? I got into the elevator and it took too
long, stopping at every floor. I wanted fresh air. I needed
out of this building.

Finally, I got off the elevator and as soon as I turned the
corner, I ran into my mom. She had no idea. I remember
she still had a look of hope on her face. The kind of hope
that only comes from not knowing. The kind of hope you
hold onto so tight because you know inevitably the truth
does come out and that hope disappears. I looked at her
and said, "She's gone. They made us turn off the machines, and now she's gone."

And I'll never forget that moment. My mom fell to her
knees and wept. We sat there in the stairwell, huddled on
the ground crying. She insisted on seeing my grandma. I
couldn't bring myself to go into the room. I wish now that I
did. But in that moment, it was too real. My mom was in
there with her for about ten minutes. I don't know what she
was doing in there, and I never asked.

When I got home I saw my grandpa sitting in his blue recliner, with her matching one empty, right next to him. The TV was off and it was eerily quiet in the house. He didn't look up when I walked in. Why should he? The only person he cared to see walk through that door wasn't going to walk through ever again. So what did he care who was coming into the house? I stood there, staring at him. I was wondering what he was thinking. He was staring at the clock. I wondered: was he looking at the clock thinking about how life was perfect at that exact time one day ago? Or was he watching the second hand tick, wondering how many more seconds, minutes, hours, days until he could be with my grandma again.

Over the next several weeks, he and I relived that night together. He would repeat the same few things:

"I shouldn't have let her work in the garden. It was so hot."

"I really wish you didn't break that clothes rack."

"What happened again? Will you tell me what happened again?"

"Why didn't she tell me she didn't feel well?"

It was strange to hear him get mad at her. He was mad that she was in the sun the day she died. It was too hot for her to be out. He was so angry at her. It was strange. Because when we get mad at one another like that, it's because we're concerned for the well-being of those we care about. We scold because we hope it'll save them from harm. Save their life. But here he was, mad at her, and it wasn't going to help. She was gone. She was never gonna come back. We can't tell her not to miss her pills. We can't tell her to get out of the sun. None of it will help now. It's done. She's done.

As my grandpa replayed the day of her death, getting madder that he didn't make her stay inside from the hot, Oklahoma sun, I went down my own path of torture. I couldn't forgive myself for not doing CPR. What was I so afraid of? If I'd given her CPR, her brain wouldn't have been deprived of oxygen for so long and she might still be with us. Why was I so afraid?

My grandfather died five years later. And I was very happy to see him pass. I don't know what happens when we die, where we go, if we go. But I like to believe they are together again in some kind of heaven. After my grandma died, Grandpa went into a slow deterioration. His will to live diminished every day. So the day he died, I felt a sense of comfort and relief. I lived with such guilt that I couldn't save his wife. I was given the chance to save her life, but instead I froze.

I like to think he isn't lonely and sad anymore. That they are together somewhere. And I hope they forgive me. I'm so sorry I couldn't save her. I'm so sorry I wasn't strong enough to do the right thing. And I'm so, so sorry I didn't say good night. If I could just have one more chance to do things differently. Unfortunately, a time machine hasn't been invented yet. But when it is, I know exactly where I'm going.

chapter nineteen

princess leia tweets *star wars*

Gonna be near Tatooine this weekend if anyone knows a good Thai place.

a long time ago from a galaxy far, far away

Can I just say: why do I always have to be the keeper of the important shit!!? For the record I DO NOT have the secret rebel plans. **#yuckydeathstar**

a long time ago from a galaxy far, far away

Help me @ObiWanRulz. **#yuckydeathstar**

a long time ago from Super Duper Power Twitter

No, seriously, @ObiWanRulz u r like my only hope. **#yuckydeathstar**

a long time ago from Super Duper Power Twitter

Electronic lips sealed, eh **@R2Legit2Quit?**

a long time ago from Super Duper Power Twitter

Ugh. Told @GRANDESTMOFF I recognized his foul stench when I came on board. Actually recognized his foul stench from a million light yrs away! **#yuckydeathstar**

a long time ago from Teeny Tiny Twitter

@MouthBreathingMenace we are so going to rock u like a hurricane plus X-wing fighters. **#yuckydeathstar**

a long time ago from Teeny Tiny Twitter

RT @MouthBreathingMenace *I sense something, a presence I've not felt since . . .* Scared much!? Suck my left one!

a long time ago from Teeny Tiny Twitter

Remind me: the best way to get peanut sauce stains out of a blindingly white shirt/dress thingie?

a long time ago from Teeny Tiny Twitter

Good recommendation btw @ObiWanRulzl Really tasty gai town kha . . . thx.

a long time ago from Teeny Tiny Twitter

Sleeping in this cell is wreaking havoc on my 'do. No stupid jokes, please! Heard them all before.
a long time ago from Teeny Tiny Twitter

@yodadude—yep even the one about looking like a bagel sandwhich with extra pastrami. U suck!:]]
a long time ago from Teeny Tiny Twitter

Ah, much better. Freedom! U rule @WompRatKilla!
a long time ago from Teeny Tiny Twitter

OK OMFG, ROFL @yodadudem, LMFAO, GOOD 1, BTW WTF @ C3POMYGAWD!?
a long time ago from Teeny Tiny Twitter

@C3POMYGAWD is giving me 'droid rage! Heehee.
a long time ago from Teeny Tiny Twitter

Crazy town! Totally want to "use the force" on @WompRatKilla. Weird!
a long time ago from Teeny Tiny Twitter

Yes @Flyingsolo I *would* call that a disturbance in the force!
a long time ago from Teeny Tiny Twitter

Nice blaster holder @Flyingsolo.
a long time ago from Teeny Tiny Twitter

Not being snarky @Flyingsolo, swear!Also, sweet ride (http://bit.ly/2m1jYg)!
a long time ago from Teeny Tiny Twitter

But WTF?: RT @walkingcarpet *graawwwwahhwwaaaa*
a long time ago from Teeny Tiny Twitter

@WompRatKilla who? Bring on @ Flyingsolo! Wait, what??? I know!
a long time ago from Teeny Tiny Twitter

Ha! RT @Flyingsolo *boring conversation anyway.* Love it! #yuckydeathstar
a long time ago from Teeny Tiny Twitter

Smellllllllllllllly!
a long time ago from Teeny Tiny Twitter

Um, @Flyingsolo—lay off my caboose, huh?
a long time ago from Teeny Tiny Twitter

RT @WompRatKilla *Nooooooooooooooooo.* **Sigh.**
a long time ago from Teeny Tiny Twitter

Hey @ ObiWanRulz you nailed the Thai food so thought I'd ask: could really use some of your mind tricks up in here, ya know? bc, yo, my mind is playing tricks on me, lol! #yuckydeathstar
a long time ago from a galaxy far, far away

Looking for a good dry cleaner. Thanks all of space!
a long time ago from a galaxy far, far away

Double ha! RT @Flyingsolo *You're all clear kid! Now let's blow this thing and go home!* **Um . . . any questions @MouthBreathingMenace?**
a long time ago from a galaxy far, far away

Oh, wait, @MouthBreathingMenace, I forgot—you can't tweet when your TIE fighter is f'ed! Yeah, sorry about that . . . I guess! #yuckydeathstar
a long time ago from a galaxy far, far away

For once I have to say I agree with you @walkingcarpet RT *graawwwwahhwwaaaa.* **Indeed. #yuckydeathstar**
a long time ago from a galaxy far, far away

Okay, @WompRatKilla, @Flyingsolo, @ObiWanRulz, @yodadude, @walkingcarpet and yes, @C3POMYGAWD and @R2Legit2Quit—party at my pad! #yuckydeathstar
a long time ago from Super Duper Power Twitter

And nice work especially @WompRatKilla and @Flyingsolo. You guys are totally getting necklaces or something!
a long time ago from Super Duper Power Twitter

Gross @Flyingsolo! I most certainly will not do *that.* **You'll be lucky to get a peck on the cheek. Ew!**
a long time ago from Super Duper Power Twitter

chapter twenty

random true story #2

Once I was at the

Sundance Film Festival in Park City, Utah, and was invited to a celebrity snowboarding event. A ton of celebrities—some famous, some not— gathered at a restaurant and scored a bunch of free shit, which is basically why people go to Sundance now.

I was getting dressed in my free snowboard gear before going, um, snowboarding, and noticed someone looking at me. He was a black guy with dreads, sunglasses and a mouth filled with gold—what I believe the kids refer to as a "grill." Awesome.

So this guy approached and said hello. I returned his hello and then asked with what can only be described as a very young, very white and very stupid-sounding voice: "Are you Lil Wayne?"

He stared for a second, looked not incredibly psyched. Then he responded: "No."

An awkward beat went by and then I asked in the same young, stupid, white-girl voice:

"Are you Lil . . . Somethin'?"

Again, not psyched: "Lil *Jon*."

Riiiight. I knew he was "Lil" something . . . I just couldn't figure out which Lil he was.

Lil Jon. Got it.

An honest mistake. Right?

Kthxbye!

chapter twenty-one

"masturbatory" is not always a metaphor in hollywood

There are certain

sentences one never expects to actually hear in real life. "What's your sign?" comes to mind. So does "Wow, what a satisfying televised political dialogue and exchange of ideas I just saw." Might you hear such things in a lame Hollywood movie or in the douchie fantasy world of some C-list starlet or Meghan McCain? Sure. But not in *real life*. Right?

Not so fast.

"Don't you know who I am?" was exactly what I heard uttered by a slobby, fat, smug and ridiculously rich and famous blockbuster film director at the very first movie premiere I attended. Was he for real with this? Apparently so.

Sure, I had been warned about Hollywood, with its egos and excesses and . . . egos. But still, that hadn't prepared me for the sheer, openly assholic behavior of many of its less classy denizens. How does one even answer a question like that? And is it meant to be rhetorical? A linguistic lasso deployed to rope you into their sadly screwed-up existence? Who knows? All I know is this is what popped out of my mouth upon hearing the question: "No, I'm sorry."

Okay, yes, I lied. And you know what? It felt great. Of course I knew who the son of a bitch in front of me was—anyone who has sat through a billion-dollar popcorn movie in the past ten years would—but I sure as hell was not about to give him the satisfaction of knowing that I knew, much less fawning over his tubby little self. So I lied. If it hurt anyone it was this guy—and he clearly deserved it. Sure, he'd earned a bit of fuck-you money over the years—but did that give him a license to douchify? I think not.

"No, I'm sorry." Ha! That flicker of panic in his squinty eyes made it all so worth it.

Cut to a few months later. By then I had settled into life in L.A.—and by settled I mean I was still renting a couch for

$400 a month from a pair of selfish and fabulously gay cousins who hearted wearing my new, expensive heels until the seams burst. Luckily, I was busy with my career and going on regular auditions, which got me out of the house a lot. And that's also where I met most of my new Hollywood friends. One such friend was this nice, blond, Midwestern guy named Jim. One night Jim invited me and a bunch of other actors out to a movie premiere. I jumped at the chance.

If you've ever watched a Discovery Channel documentary on cheetahs, say, or animals living wild in the jungle, you basically have seen what a Hollywood premiere is like. It's a mad scrum where the Hollywood correspondents wield microphones like sharp claws and attempt to corner and then feast on the flesh of the more powerful lions and tigers and bears—oh, hells yeah! It's actually pretty exciting, what with all the glamorous people craning toward the frenzied paparazzi, who flash away, the camera bulbs popping until it looks like a scene out of *Raging Bull.*

It was while elbowing my way into the crowd that I saw Jim and flagged him down. He told me he was working on a new movie and invited me down to the set the next day. Perfect! Well, almost—Jim worked as an assistant to Mr. "Do You Know Who I Am?" himself! *Nooooooooooooooooo!*

I had thought a movie premiere was exciting but it's got nothing on a movie set. Like, really amazing. I pulled up to the set the following day and took stock of the scene: we were inside an airplane hangar meant to look like a gorgeous beach house. Movie magic, yo! The lead actress—small, busty A-list walking paparazzi bait—hid behind enormous shades. So did the male lead, a guy who had parlayed an incredibly successful TV career as a bumbling charmer into a film career playing bumbling charmers. I made a mental note to call my mom as soon as possible, as she absolutely adored his work.

And holy crap—here he was totally talking to me. Or at least he said, "Hello," and flashed a blindingly white smile. That was a hell of a lot more than the lead actress had done to acknowledge me—well, in fairness, she had sent a flurry of mental daggers my way when I'd overheard her asking an assistant if any of the pretty girls on set were prettier than her.

Actor dude, by comparison, seemed so human, so normal. He even wanted to speak with me more—how sweet! "Can you get me a water? It's Fiji, room temperature. But you should know that by now."

Ugh. He thought I was his *assistant*. Really?! He talks to his assistant that way? What an asshole. Not wanting to cause a stink or mess up the shoot I bit my tongue and ran off in search of his stupid bottle of water.

Jim helped me get over the whole horrible incident by bringing me down to "video village," where all the most important people on the set hung out. Suddenly I was sitting with the director—yes, *that* director—the producers, and the script supervisor. Who the hell was I? This was so f'ing cool.

Then the love scene they were shooting started and . . .

"Cut!"yelled the director as he hopped off his chair. "This scene needs more goddamn romance." At which point he waddled over to the lovemaking bed, undid his jeans—I could already sense that those must be the hardest-working buttons in show business—and proceeded to dry hump the actress in order to demonstrate what he believed was the missing level of romance.

The poor thing—her face sparkled with the sweat falling from his second or third chin. When he finally finished the assault he barked, "Let's take twenty!" I'm pretty sure it would take a lot longer than that for his starlet to recover from the trauma.

The crew dispersed—production assistants fondled their walkie-talkies, key grips wandered off in search of a quick beer and craft services prepped for the ravenous hordes to lunch. Jim was out of his head busy so he asked me to deliver a "diet plate" to the director's trailer. I was eager to help a new friend in any way I could. "No problem," I chirped. No way I could've known then how wrong I was.

I knocked on the screen door to the trailer and when no response came I tiptoed in. No one was around so I gently put down the high-fiber, protein-rich, calorically correct plate of food and turned to go. That's when I noticed an already mauled additional plate of grub that looked like a meal made to feed most of the hungriest parts of Africa. A half-eaten tub of lasagna. A mangled basket of garlic bread. Other chewed-up carb bits. And then also: the loneliest untouched plate of vegetables ever prepared for a gluttonous bastard. The whole thing was just—ew.

I shuddered and began tiptoeing back out of the disaster zone that was his trailer. And then I heard, "Why so fast?"

I turned and confronted a waking nightmare: fresh from the toilet, The Director emerged with jeans buttons bursting, swooped up the "diet plate" and disappeared into the back of the trailer. Did I really just see that? I'm afraid I had. Now out of view, I could still hear him gobbling and slobbering up the "diet plate," which was obviously one serious misnomer. I turn to walk out and then the beast called out, "Come in here."

"Thanks," I offered meekly, "but I really should go."

And that's when it happened again: "Don't you know who I am?" He ticked off a few of his bigger box-office blockbusters, hoping to jog my memory. I couldn't help myself:

"Uh, no, sorry, doesn't ring a bell."

"Nope. Never saw it."

"Oh, yeah, saw the trailer for that one. But, no. Didn't see it."

I turned again to leave.

"Wait," he begged.

Slowly, like in a bad horror movie, I turned around once more. And I remember first noticing him wearing an Oxford shirt and holding a fistful of cocktail sauce–smothered shrimp. He popped one down his throat and then another and another, the red sauce collecting like so much baby's blood at the corner of his smirking mouth before dribbling down his front and settling as glistening stains on his shirt.

As if in competition with himself to drop all the worst lines on me at once, in order to win the Douche Olympics or something, this A-list schmuck then has the nerve to say: "You have such an interesting look—what ethnicity are you?"

He was masturbating. Right there. With shrinp in one hand. And me standing in front of him.

Again: Was he for real? All too real, I'm afraid. Because—and this is where things crossed over from merely disturbing to downright horrific—that was the exact moment I noticed what was either a tiny gnarled doggie toy or this adult man's penis being stroked by his own stubby hand. The winner and still champion! Douche Gold would be his! I mean—*what the fucking fuck?!!*

He was masturbating. Right there. With shrimp in one hand. And me standing in front of him. Masturbating. Mastur-bating. I'm not even kidding.

And dude was going for it, too, furiously pulling at the tragic stub. Before I could even begin to make sense of the whole deal, he was moaning, moaning and then—fire hose.

On steroids. The Mt. Saint Helens of man-juice. An eruption the size of which Los Angeles County had never before had the misfortune of bearing witness to. I am not being hyperbolic when I report to you with no small measure of dismay that this slob's cum hung from the ceiling. I could see it made its way to the stereo and draped over the buttons. Collateral damage had even claimed the doorknob, which was so integral to my escape and, thus, my sanity.

In terms of thinking on my feet this may have been among my proudest moments: there was nothing to say so I didn't bother trying; instead, I quickly located a Taco Bell wrapper, threw it around my hand, and reached for the doorknob.

For all I know the director was calling out for me to stay longer but I didn't hear a thing. Athletes sometimes talk about being in the Zone, when time slows down and they are able to focus on the task at hand with inhuman levels of concentration. Nailing a three-point shot at the buzzer. Tossing a sixty-five-yard strike in the fourth quarter of a tie ball game. Crushing a hanging curve with the bases loaded. When it comes to fleeing cocktail-sauce-stained, half-naked, masturbating Hollywood big shots, I was in the Zone. Before I knew what had happened I was through the screen door to the other side, leaning safely against the wide side of the trailer—freedom.

We've all heard tales of the debauchery and Rome-like orgies that take place in eternally flesh-loving Los Angeles.

For the hedonistic, there is no shortage of three-way, four-way, or even five-way action that can be had. There is no want of coke- and hooker-fueled parties to attend. We know this. And yet . . . and yet, nothing really can prepare you for confronting what I had just seen. A grown man in an oversized shirt holding his undersized manhood in hands glistening with shrimp fat. Not to put too fine a point on it. I had looked into the face of my own blockbuster-making Kurtz—and you know what? I'd survived. Not only that, I felt very much intact. After the dust settled and I had a moment to analyze the day's myriad disturbances, it occurred to me that I hadn't actually been shocked by anything I had seen. Appalled? Sure. Disgusted? You bet. But not shocked. And this idea gave me comfort. In an odd way it was comforting to know that people you imagine are oversexed, misogynistic pigs are, in fact, oversexed, misogynistic pigs. It made me realize that sometimes people are *exactly* who you expect them to be.

chapter twenty-two
spotting assholes made easy

Assholes—they're everywhere.
But how to spot 'em? It might be a trickier
question to answer than you'd think. Consider
a famous asshole like Bill Clinton. At first blush
you might think he was a cool motherfucker,
right? Like, as president, Clinton totally got us
out of major debt and oversaw an unprece-
dented modern era of peace and prosperity.
Plus he seems to really care about poor
people.

And yet . . . and yet . . . hotheaded assholes, the both of them.

The truth is, you never *really* know when you might be surrounded by assholes (unless you are at the Hollywood club *du jour*, in which case you can be sure you are absolutely neck deep in them—what a relief to know!). There might be one lurking in your bed AT THIS VERY MOMENT! Or under the couch. Or playing skeeball. And there is certainly one on the TV right now.

The truth is, you never *really* know when you might be surrounded by assholes.

How do I know? I just do. Some people have great gaydar; me, I'm lucky enough to have superior assdar (holedar?). So as a public service I've compiled the following list of ways you too can spot an asshole. There are surely many, many more ways than the ones I've noted here, but this is a good start. Clip it and save!

1. Drivers who don't do the "thanks for letting me in wave" when you let them in.

2. People who give you gifts for your home and get pissed if you don't display it every day of your life.

3. Someone who texts in the theater.

4. Observe the cell phone holster on some fella's belt and look up at the person wearing it.

5. Any guy who doesn't at least pretend to reach for his wallet when the check comes (see pg. 135 for more on this).

6. Any guy who interrupts and answers questions meant for his wife/girlfriend/girl you're fucking.

7. Any guy who quotes *Napoleon Dynamite* too often and acts like no one has ever done that before. You know who you are.

8. A guy who decides what to do in his life by saying aloud, "What would Paul Newman do?"

9. Anyone who decries something by saying it's "totally gay."

10. Anyone who is rude to people in the service industry.

11. If he throws toast at the wall just because they forgot the jelly.

12. People who don't like pie.

13. If the guy in front of you at Starbucks takes more than fifteen seconds to communicate his drink order, then guess what? Good spotting!

14. Dick Cheney.

15. Walking around with Bluetooth without a hint of embarrassment.

16. People who force their pets to wear clothes.

17. People who don't say their name when you meet them.

18. Meteorologists.

19. Accidental transvestites/hipsters wearing insanely tight jeans.

20. Someone who constantly looks around for someone better to talk to.

21. People who drive a Prius and act like they're doing something more to save the world than you.

22. Middle-aged ponytail wearers who are not Johnny Depp.

23. Chronic salad eaters.

24. People who honk their horns *the freaking second* the light turns green.

25. Jabba the Hutt.

chapter twenty-three

boys can be really great—
and also really f'ing annoying

I probably don't need

to say this but I will anyway: I love boys. I grew up with two brothers and around lots of male cousins and friends. Now I very much enjoy kissing boys and I often get to third base and even farther.

But that doesn't excuse the fact that—and this is a true fact—they can annoy the crap out of me sometimes. You know why? Because they can be . . . well, annoying as crap.

So if you are a boy reading this and we ever get to hang out, please keep the following things in mind and please, for the love of all that is sacred, try to avoid them:

1. DO NOT BECOME A WHINEY BITCH WHEN YOU GET SICK.
Why do boys always turn into such babies when they're sick? It really is unbelievable. I was dating a guy once where every time he got sick I prayed for the sweet release of death. He would get sick and immediately start whining and crying for things.

Why do boys always turn into such babies when they're sick?

"Can I get some soup . . . I'm sick. Can you turn on the TV . . . I'm sick. Can you bring me another blanket . . . I'm sick. Can you create a time machine so I don't get so bored . . ."

It never stopped. Men—correction, boys—almost literally grow a vagina the minute their temperature hits ninety-nine degrees. I don't understand it. One minute my boyfriend is working out, smoking weed, drinking scotch . . . the next he can't even get his own fucking water and needs lavender-scented candles to "relax his spirit." Yeah, okay—I understand that when anyone is sick they like to be babied and taken care of. So then, what happens when a dude's girlfriend gets sick? Caring, understanding, returning the same kind of attentive treatment the girlfriend just gave? Yeaaaah . . . No. They freak out. First, they insist you're not sick.

"It's just in your head. You're just tired. You need to exercise and get some more energy. Even better? We should go skydiving since you're staying home from work anyway."

What!? I'm sick. Remember when I brought in the space heater and rubbed your feet for TWO hours while you lay in bed watching a *Sober House* marathon? Or how you insisted that I make all of your EmergenC drinks with a straw because it hurt to bend your neck to drink? Yet, when I'm sick we're jumping out of a motherfucking plane? When they finally realize that I am actually, truly ill, then they become too afraid to be in the same Zip code practically.

"Okay, honey. Stay in the room, in bed and if you need anything . . . anything at all, call my cell and I'll put it outside the door."

Um . . . thanks?

2. DON'T TALK LIKE AN ASSHOLE. Okay. I know this might not apply to all boys, but it does to a good amount that I've met in recent years. And it goes something like this:

"All hands on deck!"

"It's really blowing up!"

"Let's kick things into gear!"

"It's better to give than receive."

Sure, all common sayings. But most people use really popular sayings—that is, clichés—in jest. No one really uses them seriously.

Sadly, I've heard so many boys use them completely unironically in regular conversation. My friend recently signed a new contract at his work and was also developing some new projects. In his excitement he actually said, "It's about to be really huge—I'm talking 'all hands on deck right now.'" I had to laugh a little. Really? People talk like that? I guess so.

Another time this guy at work made an Internet video and I overheard him telling another coworker, "Yeah, you should totally check it out. It's really blowing up on the Internet right now." Okay: You are not allowed to be the one saying that your shit is blowing up. (Note: If your shit is truly blowing up, you don't have to tell someone.) The best part about this statement was how casually it was dropped. "Oh you know, I just fucked a supermodel, whatever, not a big deal . . . wanna grab lunch?" Classic. Totally pimp yourself but act like it's not a big deal. Sure, no one will see past that.

This time, I couldn't help myself and actually asked, "Did you really just say 'it's blowing up on the Internet'?" He blushed and walked away. I guess it doesn't sound so cool and casual when you hear someone else say it. And yet I'm pretty sure I overheard him say *the exact same thing* like an hour later to someone else! WTF!?

Then there's the time-tested double up. That's when a guy says the same line twice as if they came up with it themselves. So, like, you're pissed that your sister forgot your birthday even though she shares your same birthday . . . and you say:

"Hey, it's always better to give than receive . . . (Long pause to make sure you're taking it in and also to make it seem like he came up with it, partnered with an intense look in his eyes, then repeat.) "It's better to give (pause for dramatic effect) . . . than receive."

Okaaaay . . . are we really pretending you made up that quote, Bartlett? Or are we agreeing that you didn't make it up, but you feel that after all these years of hearing teachers say that in elementary school, it's finally sinking in because you're saying it with such a dramatic pause?

Bottom line: only time it's acceptable to use such hoary clichés is when you're trying to be funny or lame. And you really have to be trying.

3. HAVE A MÉNAGE À TROIS ALREADY. A boyfriend told me once, "Having a threesome for a guy is like doing anal— everyone's done it, and if you haven't done it, you need to." Men are obsessed with having threesomes. They just can't get it out of their heads (pun intended . . . hehe). If you've ever dated a guy who hasn't had a threesome, it's so incredibly annoying. It's like dating a dirty virgin. All he can talk about is how all of his friends have done it and he feels left out. What's worse than dating a threesome virgin?

Dating a guy who got *thisclose* to a threesome but either chickened out at the last minute or was interrupted and couldn't complete the act. Why is it worse? Because he just won't stop talking about it and reliving the moment with every detail in hopes that you might hear it, turn into a fairy godmother and grant him the wish of finishing that story. Then, all the questions come in:

"Would you ever do a threesome? Which one of your friends would you most likely do a threesome with? Who's the hottest girl you know? Would you ever kiss a girl?"

Then as he starts to realize you're not taking the bait, the questions get really pathetic:

"Okay, if we have a threesome—and I'm just saying 'if' because you never know what tomorrow will bring (another annoying damn saying!!) . . . you never know . . . what to-morrow will bring (with the dramatic pause!!!) . . . would you be cool if I just fucked you while you go down on her? Okay, okay . . . what if I don't even touch her but I get to watch the two of you make out? Okay, okay, okay . . . what if . . . ummm . . . I fuck you and then you two just braid each other's hair?"

My advice? Have a damn threesome. Like, now. If you get the opportunity, do it. And they don't have to be hot. They just have to be born with a vagina, still be in posses-sion of said vagina and you have to have sex with both of them. Don't get bogged down in details like their looks and stuff—just get the threesome out of the way! Like Kanye says, "They might be fives but together they're a ten."

And do it before you get with a girl you really want to settle down with. Because—trust me on this one—it's very, very hard to find a girl that you'd want to take home to Mom, have a meaningful relationship with and possibly bear your children, who will also finger-bang another girl while you do her doggy-style. Get it done. Get it out of the way. If you don't do it, you will regret it and never move past it. You will be the new virgin. And no one wants that, especially your girlfriend.

chapter twenty-four

here's the part about moving to oklahoma, throwing my first party, and fake sleeping to trick the cops

I moved from Japan

to Oklahoma when I was sixteen years old. Yeah, exactly, great time to move to a completely new school. Most people ask me if living in Japan was hard. But the truth is that living in Oklahoma was the hardest place I've ever lived. The thing about living in Oklahoma, or any part of the Midwest, is that people grow up together from kindergarten on. So when I come to this new school as a junior, it was like walking onto the set of *Degrassi High* or some shit. Oh, and in this season of *Degrassi*, I wasn't even a regular character; I was more like the weird girl who occasionally gets a bone thrown her way in the form of a line or two. And then dies of some terminal disease.

What made my transition to the school even harder was that I had come from a school in Japan where, after a year of struggling through the typical high school hazing bullshit, I had somehow climbed my way to the teeny top. What does it mean to be at the top in high school? People actually stopped to say hi to me. They wouldn't move away when I sat next to them in the cafeteria. Seemingly normal things when you look back as an adult, but back then, it meant *everything* to me. But now, in this foreign land called "Oklahoma," no one knew me. No one saw me.

Now I should explain my look at this time in my life. Back then trends in Japan, were like four or five years behind. So at this point, I was in the alternative "skater" phase. I wore men's big baggy jeans, with Converse sneakers, men's T-shirts and my hair parted down the middle and hanging halfway in my face. I looked like the saddest Chili Peppers' roadie. And what was the prevalent style in Oklahoma? Preppy. Insanely preppy. Gap sweater vests and cargo shorts and button ups, striped Polos and clean white sneakers. Oh, and one more thing to complete the picture of me as the absolute outsider? I didn't wear any makeup. I was modeling and cheerleading in Japan so I already had enough people putting makeup on me, and I didn't want to wear it in my everyday life. So, I never wore any makeup. And the Oklahoma girls, well, I'm pretty sure they were born with a curling iron in their hand. They had it all—

beautiful faces slathered in mascara, hair perfectly curled, draped in the perfect little preppy outfits. Somehow I'd wandered into a freaking Ralph Lauren photo shoot dressed like Pete Wentz or a Madden brother. Sweet!

The first month of school was almost unbearable for me. I would walk through the halls in my big baggy jeans and oversized shirt, and look around. I was hoping to make eye contact with someone. Anyone. Any recognition that they actually *saw* me. I cried for the entire first month I was at that school. Every morning I would pull into the parking lot in my maroon Honda Accord with every intention of making friends and having a great day. But as soon as I walked through the front doors, I would smell that familiar waft of cafeteria rolls baking and hear the indecipherable chatter and gossip of people who were around me every day, yet did not even know I was alive. The combination of those two senses would bring something up inside me that no matter how hard I prayed to suppress it, would force tears to pour out of my eyes. You know how at *Cheers* everyone knows your name and you get free mugs of beer? I just thought I'd mention that so you could under-stand how *not* like *Cheers* my life was like at that moment.

I would walk the hallway to first period, crying. I would sit down in first period crying. We would begin class and I would stop crying. I would look up at the clock and count only five more minutes until the bell would ring and I would

be forced back out in the hall . . . I started crying. And it went on like that for every period, every day for a month.

One day I decided I wasn't going to wallow in this pity anymore. I had, after all, managed to persevere through the brutality of every new school I'd attended. After all those years, I had to have learned something about adapting. So I stopped being sad and started thinking about what I could do to make friends. First things first—I noticed I wasn't dressing like the girls at all. I immediately went and applied for a job at The Gap. I figured I could get discounts on a whole new wardrobe and also make new friends with my Friends and Family discount! Great plan. I'm nothing if not a problem solver, right? I bought some cargo shorts, a button-up jeans shirt and white Keds. Then I looked at what group I wanted to hang out with. I noticed a sign for students to sign up and make banners for the weekend football game. Pep Squad? I like pep. Sounds fun. Honestly, at this point, it didn't

And that's how I found myself sitting in the driveway of some girl's house, painting stars onto a banner.

matter who they were, I just wanted one friend. I mean, for God's sake, I was so pathetic, my older sister used to drive forty-five minutes from her college just to have lunch with me, so I wouldn't have to sit by myself. Seriously, anyone would do. The only requirement was they had to have a pulse and even that was negotiable. (Oh, and not have bad breath. I draw the line with bad breath.)

And that's how I found myself sitting in the driveway of some girl's house, painting stars onto a banner. I was wearing my cargo shorts and striped two-button shirt. Everyone was nice but not really talking to me. Then one girl turned to me and said, "Great cargos!" I was so excited. I was noticed and my outfit worked! I asked her if she wanted to go to The Gap and use my discount. She said she'd call me. Yes! (Note: She never did call me, the preppy skank.)

After that I went through a very strange period. Almost every month I would join a new clique. But not just join them, I would completely transform myself. And this is not an exaggeration AT. ALL. Let me walk you through the months:

Month 1: Student Government clique—sweater vest, American flag pin, jeans, and white Keds.

Month 2: Cheerleaders—sweatpants, Asics cheerleading shoes (I still had mine from my last school), high school mascot T-shirt and hair pulled into a ponytail, wrapped with ribbon.

Month 3: Alternative, potheads—lots of chains, black nail polish, black lipstick, and anything from Hot Topic.

Month 4: The Librarians—the 70-year-old librarian ladies! We would share our lunches and read. I would wear conservative clothing and lots of button-up sweaters.

Month 5: Debate—Blazer, jeans, white Oxford.

Month 6: Athletes—Track pants (the kind that swish loudly as you walk) and matching jacket.

Also **Month 6:** Partiers, popular group—Levi jeans, boots, fitted shirts and water bra (yes, these are in fact what you think they are. Instead of padding, it's filled with a water/gel substance so it feels real if I guy feels me up over the shirt).

The "popular" group was the group I always wanted to be in. Guilty as charged: I wanted to fit in; I wanted to be popular. I know that it's horrible to admit that. You can't say in high school that you "want to be popular." But now looking back I can say it. There, I said it. So many people think it's cool to say that they didn't care about being popular or they liked being an outsider. But I really do feel that most people want to be liked and loved and recognized . . . especially in high school. So to me the "popular" group meant I made it in this social status game.

Unfortunately for me, they didn't cherish my friendship as much as I did theirs. One day, I was out to lunch with a group of the popular girls. I was telling them how my mom was going away for three weeks to Vietnam. Immediately they put down their bagels and perked up.

"Where are you going to stay?" one asked.

"At home. By myself. My mom trusts me. And it's not that long," I responded.

"Oh my God! You should have a party!" one exclaimed.

Strange as it might sound, I had never considered that. I mean, in Japan we didn't have house parties. We would just go to a club or down near a river and hang out. We would never go into our parents' home and throw a party. You can't accidentally break your dad's stereo by pouring tequila all over it at the river, after all. We were, I suppose, better behaved in Japan.

Nonetheless, I agreed to the party after the other girls promised me it would just be ten, fifteen people tops. And I was excited. I was gonna make some more new friends and have a party! How "So-Called Life" of me.

The day my mom left town, a Friday, I was walking through the halls on my way to class and someone handed me a flier saying, "Party tonight. Ten bucks cover. It's gonna be sick." Sick! Awesome! Wait! WTF?!

I looked down at the paper and noticed something familiar. It was a map and directions leading directly to my house. Holy crap.

I got home that day and was really excited about how big the party had become. Sure I was also a tad nervous, but mostly I was psyched. People are coming to *my* party?! They must really like me!

This is so embarrassing, but the first thing I did was . . . I started setting up snacks. Snacks! It was a keg party with a bunch of kids from a high school who didn't know who I was and only wanted a house to get wasted in and make money on selling beer. Why the hell would they be impressed with my cheese and grapes? I was clueless and put out my trays of crackers, nuts and pretzels. Very Martha Stewart hosting *Twilight*.

The doorbell rings and it's a tall guy with long blond hair. I didn't recognize him. He closed the door and let his friend through the garage where they carried in six large kegs. After placing them around the house and backyard, the blond guy went and took his place at the door. I would later learn that he was the door guy, collecting money from every one of my new "friends" as they came in.

I was so naïve. I had no idea. I was just so happy to have a bunch of people in *my* house at *my* party. I was never a big drinker. But, that night, I was in full-on celebrating mode.

My uncle had bought thousands of dollars of stereo equipment and my mom had stored it in the living room. Before the party I threw a sheet over it. Not thinking anyone would ever intrude on my privacy. There, that oughtta do it.

At one point in the night, however, of course someone lifted the sheet to see all the badly hidden stereo equipment. And, well, yeah. They started stealing it. That's what kids do. That and drugs. Then the inevitable: cops came to bust up the party. Everyone in the house scattered like cockroaches when the lights turned on. They all raced around the house and yard and the cops tackled my friends/thieves so that they would drop the stereo boxes they were attempting to jack.

Where was I during this awesome melee? This is brilliant. As soon as we heard the cops come into the house, one helpful girl grabbed my arm and told me to go "pretend like you're sleeping." It was so stupid. But I was drunk and had no idea what was going on. So I lay down in my bed with a plan to tell the cops if they ever came to me, "Officer, I had no idea there was a party going on with underage drinking. I was sleeping the whole time. I musta really conked out. Weird." I put my head on the pillow, closed my eyes and waited. After a few minutes, I sat up and realized how thoroughly stupid that idea was. I turned on the light and heard the cops walking down the hallway. I looked around the room and noticed a massive pile of weed on my desk. In one fell swoop, I wiped the whole pile onto the floor, crushing it with my foot into the brown shag carpet.

The cops walked right past my door without even looking in. When I came out of the room, only one friend was left. We walked around the house cleaning things up and picking up stereo equipment that was scattered around the lawn. Somehow I'd survived.

Back at school Monday morning everyone was talking about the party. How it was the best party of the year. And everyone knew me! Everyone knew it was my party, my best party of the year. Yes. Mission accomplished.

Except . . . oh yeah. That's right. Nothing in my life could go according to plan. That must be why a few hours into the school day I got a call from the principal's office saying I needed to go home immediately. I arrived at my house to see two police officers with their guns drawn, pointing at my house. Seems that during class, a couple guys had broken into my house, trying to steal the boxed up stereo equipment they were forced to leave behind. They knew I would be at school and thought it was the perfect time to rob me. They didn't realize I had set the alarm on the house.

This broke my heart. I was devastated. All I wanted was to fit in and have people like me. I opened my home to these people and now they're breaking into my house and robbing me?!

The next day at school I went up to the guys I heard had done it. I confronted them and looked into their eyes. These big, macho, stoner guys couldn't even look at me. They were pathetic and disgusting. But the odd thing is, they actually ended up doing me a big favor.

I realized then that it doesn't matter how popular you are, or how great your party is or what social group you're associated with . . . none of that matters if you're sur-rounded by a bunch of people who don't give a fuck about you. A bunch of people who suck.

I wanted so badly to be on the inside. To be liked and recognized and popular. But at that very moment, I realized that none of it matters if you don't have real friends. Okay, yes, this is the after-school special lesson moment of this chapter—deal with it! Of course, in high school that is your whole world. How popular and loved you are there is how well you do in life. That's what you think because your whole life from 7 A.M. to 3 P.M. is that high school with those people. But eventually you get out of high school and you realize that all of those people don't matter. It doesn't matter what they thought of you, what you thought of them, who wore what and who drove what. Because when you're out in the real world, you can make up your own mind about whom you want to hang out with and be friends with and who's allowed at your party. And chances are, those friends won't rob you blind.

So those bastards broke my heart. But they also made me realize that I wasn't going to spend one more day trying to make these people like me. I was going to live my life for me and be friends with only the people I truly liked. I was lucky to have learned that lesson. Because my senior year in high school, although it had its fair share of boy problems and drama, was amazing. For the first time in a long time, I didn't care if anyone saw me. Because I saw myself.

chapter twenty-five
unfortunate e-mail sign-offs

1. Sent from the women's bathroom's glory hole.

2. Have a ducky day!

3. Your time is my money.

4. My body, MY choice.

5. Namaste.

6. If you like your freedom, thank a Bush!

7. This e-mail was sent from inside your house.

8. Jesus Loves You.

9. Taking care of business.

10. Sent from my iPhone.

chapter twenty-six
the day i saw
my first antique dildo

I had another friend

who was working as an assistant for some studio executive. And when I first moved to L.A., I didn't know many people and would run around with him while he did errands.

So I'm with my friend one day and he needs to drop something off for his boss at some guy's house. I didn't recognize the name but I knew he was successful by the bigger-is-better size of the houses in the neighborhood. After winding our way through the glorious, golden hills we drove through a gate, down a long driveway, past a tennis court that looked perfectly manicured but never used. The inside of the house was dark with lots of leather furniture and mahogany. There was a lot of stuff around, knickknacks, tchotchkes . . . and, like, way too many places to sit. It was weird. There was a couch, a loveseat, a chair, stool or . . . something to rest on everywhere you looked. I started to imagine that whoever lived here might not have any legs. Or they might have a really big ass. Or maybe they just really loved to take a load off. They certainly appeared to have lots of loads to take off. Anyway.

My friend said he needed to run the envelope to someone in another part of the house, but in the meantime I should, "Go in and meet him. This is his house."

Okay.

I have to tell you, and this is embarrassing, but I had no idea who the hell he was. Because as I came to find out, he is one of Hollywood's most successful producers. A while back, he worked on a handful of films that are commonly regarded as some of the best films ever made. One of them was nominated for a Best Picture Oscar. Collectively his films made wads and wads of cash. He still knows and is friends with many of the most powerful people in movies. So, yeah, not about to cross this dude.

All I knew about this man was that he sure loved himself some good sittin' and since I had absolutely nothing else to do, I might as well meet him. I was intrigued.

I walked into his master bedroom. And no, that wasn't as odd as it might sound. I quickly realized that at his age being in his bedroom was like being at lunch at The Ivy. Unlike most of us, this man does not use this bedroom just for sleeping, sex and luring young girls into his libidinous trap. Sure, he probably uses it for that, too, but also for breakfast, lunch, dinner, reading, writing, arithmetic, cutting his toenails . . . this bedroom was the world to him.

I had no idea what to expect. I see an elderly gentleman with his hair perfectly parted, wearing red silk pajamas. The blankets are pulled up around him and the bed is covered in magazines, books, a laptop, notepads and pencils. I'm introduced to him by one of his staffers and he perks up and asks me to come sit next to him on the bed. I didn't feel uncomfortable. Like I said, this was no mere sex lair. The energy was closer to an outdoor patio where everyone hangs out than an intimate boudoir.

I sat on the bed and he asked me where I was from and who my agent was. Almost immediately he goes: "No, no, no, they're good but not great. You should be with the big agencies. Give me your number and I'll make a few calls for you and get you in with the biggest agent in town."

I told him I was happy with my agent and thanked him for his offer. I think he could tell that I didn't know who he was. He went into the story of his life. Something about something, I don't remember . . . But, someone had made a critically acclaimed documentary about Hollywood, in which he figured prominately, and I should watch it because it'll show me how I, too, can become successful in Hollywood.

Then he suddenly reached over to his nightstand, opened a drawer and grabbed a copy of the DVD. Wow: so conveniently stacked to give away to every single person who walked through the door. He asked me to grab the Sharpie at the edge of the bed so he could sign it. Great. Cool. Awesome. Maybe the documentary would tell me why he liked to sit so much.

He signed the DVD and handed it back to me. I graciously

took it and smiled. "I can't wait to watch it. Thanks a lot."
He smiled and laid his head back on the pillow. Then he
said, "I want to show you one more thing."

He asked me to grab a trinket on his nightstand. I stood
up and walked around to his side of the bed. He pointed to
a little box. On the nightstand were roughly fifty different
antique boxes—most of them bronze or gold with little jew-
els on them. I noticed a picture of a famous actress who
happens to be in one of my all-time favorite movies. It
looked like they were in love. This guy used to date her?
Okay, I'm impressed. I picked up the tiny, jeweled box and
he told me to open it. I opened it and saw what looked like
a metal top. You know, one of those things you spin on the
ground and just watch . . . spin? So, it looked like a metal
top or maybe a small wine opener. My interest was piqued.
I love antiques and this was clearly some kind of music box
or toy or . . .

"What is it?" I asked excitedly.

There was half a beat, maybe less.

"You use it to masturbate with," he responded.

I wasn't sure I heard him correctly.

"What?" I asked.

"Women used to use it to masturbate with . . . I've used
that little box on so many women and it can really make
you happy. Go ahead, it's a gift."

Now, I'm not the kind of person who's surprised by

much in life. I've been through a lot. But this, well, this stunned me. I mean, I'm sitting here holding an antique— what, dildo? And it must have been put up the vaginal canal of a third of Hollywood at least, women who are now so old their vaginas are dry and crusty. Like they'd be sold as day-old goods in the bakery of vaginas. Then something else even more disturbing strikes me: I'm likely holding the magical dildo box that was once used on or by my big-screen heroine. Her lady parts? Noooooo.

> **I mean, I'm sitting here holding an antique— what, dildo?**

"No, thank you. I'm good," I said.

I put the box back on the table of what I realized then was probably just fifty antique dildo contraptions, said good-bye and headed out the door. I was one step outside of the bedroom before he called out to me, "Don't forget your DVD!"

I turned around, scooped up my signed copy of his life story, thanked him again for having me in his home, then went into the foyer and sat on the second leather rocking chair I saw and tried to rock myself out of a state of shock. Aha! Maybe that's why there were so many places to sit.

chapter twenty-seven
i did it all for the love of pie

Of all the All-American

things there are—baseball, freedom, Arnold Schwarzenegger—pie is by far the most delicious. A buttery, flakey, slightly browned crust is filled with vanilla pudding, bananas sliced into coins and topped with whipped cream right out of a can. That is exactly how I want my pie. And I want it a lot. My love for pie is not a mystery. But how it bonded me to fans in such a serious way that to this day—I still get a few hundred dollars' worth of pie gift certificates every year—is. Let's try to get to the bottom of it! Yay, the bottom!

I have always had a love of pie. Not in a freaky, *American Pie* way, but in an obsessed, normal way. That is, I've always loved pie like anyone else—I wanted it during holidays, on special events, and most Tuesdays. Okay, maybe I did love it a little more than most. Instead of birthday cakes growing up, I insisted on five pumpkin pies—three for me personally and two for family and friends to share. Wow—reading that out loud makes me sound like the saddest little fat kid around. But I promise I wasn't. I just really loved pie.

Eventually I grew out of my pie phase—just as with Luke Perry I learned that everything is a phase. Well, I thought it was a phase, anyway. But then, one fateful day a few years ago, I was having lunch at Marie Callender's and noticed a selection of pies on the right side of the menu. And there were pictures, too. Chocolate cream with whipped cream, banana cream with meringue, fresh strawberry topped with whipped cream—the list went on and on. A pie for every feeling, and there is a season, turn, turn . . . er . . . my bad—"Every pie for every *moment.*" It was hot steamy pie porn action for families!

I chose the chocolate cream pie with the meringue topping. It was—how to put this gracefully?—fucking orgasmic. (And as the first of a series of apologies in this chapter, let me now say sorry to the staff of Marie Callender's for the unfortunate loud moaning that took place that afternoon and any bodily secretions I may have inadvertently left on the seat.)

Every day for about a month after that, I went thirty minutes out of my way to get a piece of pie. One day I decided to ask how much an entire pie was—just for price comparison! Well, turns out an entire pie was twelve bucks and one piece of pie was like six dollars. And it just so happens that day I wanted two pieces of pie. So you don't have to be a superstar "mathlete" to figure out what was the smarter and more economic thing to do. So I did it.

The night I bought the whole pie I was having friends over for dinner. While everyone began eating the roasted chicken and vegetables, I excused myself and snuck into the kitchen. I opened the refrigerator and took out the pie. I cut two pieces and in the privacy of my own kitchen, with five friends in the other room eating a sensible dinner, I horked down two pieces of banana cream pie as fast as I could. Multiple orgasms. And no one was any wiser.

To tell you the truth, I never thought there was anything wrong with that. I'm an adult. And if I'd rather have pie for dinner, then I don't have to answer to anyone. Can we all agree on that? But I suppose the issue wasn't that I chose the pie over fresh vegetables. The problem was that I was secretly inhaling pie and I didn't want anyone to know about it. Like a crack addict, I was hiding my addiction. And this actually may have been more difficult than hiding a crack addiction because of the slurping, *nom nom nom* sounds emanating from my kitchen—and because crack doesn't leave frothing, chocolatey swirls all over your face.

After about a month of my pie binge I started noticing certain side effects—for starters, I couldn't button my jeans. Why did it take me a month to realize this? Juicy sweatpants. And I was not alone. Juicy Couture sweatpants have ruined more women than Jack Nicholson. Seriously, look around at all the girls who used to be skinny. They're all wearing leggings or jumpsuits. It's the only way you can truly be in denial about your weight gain. Stretchy pants fit everyone! So even when you're turning into a fatty, like I was, you can still feel sexy. See how they get us? Clever!

On *Attack of the Show* we often take questions from fans, and one day a fan asked, "How do you stay in such great shape?" My co-host, Kevin Pereira, answered that he works out and eats right. Good answer. And as he was answering I tried to decide what I would say. There's the classic Hollywood answer: "Oh, I eat whatever I want and it just falls off—I guess it's just good genes." Then there's the real answer. I guess I was just so sick of a lot of these Hollywood role models creating unrealistic body images. Because the answer isn't just genes. It's makeup, wardrobe, Spanx, Adderall, anorexia, bulimia. These super-skinny starlets don't eat junk food and then wish it away. So here I am, faced with this simple question. And I want to give an honest answer.

"The truth is," I started, "I've been eating so much pie lately, I can't even button my jeans." And I lifted up my shirt and showed my size twenty-five jeans unbuttoned, and my belly busting through.

The reaction I got from fans was both entirely unexpected and immediate. By the end of our show, five pies had been delivered from across the street. Fans had seen my confession and called in pies to be delivered to the studio.

Since then I've received probably about a thousand bucks' worth of pie gift certificates and whenever I go somewhere and meet fans, I get, like, ten hand-delivered pies.

All of this pie love eventually led to my desserting coup de grace: About two years ago I leaped into a massive chocolate cream pie when nearly 70,000 fans signed a petition to try to make a National Pie Week. And yes, it was my idea to jump into the pie. And yes, it was my idea to do it dressed as a French maid. Hey, we did it for the cause!

The pie crust was actually an eight-foot swimming pool that we had to drive to Bakersville, California, to secure. In order to construct this sweet monstrosity we went through twenty-four tubs and $2,500 worth of Cool Whip. The estimated weight of the pie was about 4,000 pounds.

National Pie Day (totally a real holiday, yo, and it's on January 23) was coming up. At some point in preparing for the show that day one of the producers turned to me and asked if I had any ideas to celebrate the holiday. You mean, any ideas other than eating a shitload of pie, I wanted to say. Instead, just off the top of my head I suggested possibly asking fans to sign a petition to amp it up to National Pie Week! And if we succeeded in this noble effort, I would jump into a giant pie. I didn't think about the consequences or press or pie lodged into places it shouldn't be. (Use your imagination—no, wait, don't!) It was just an innocent suggestion that I expected to get shot down in favor of a good old-fashioned pie-eating contest or something. Silly me. Silly, destined for a giant pie me.

The next day at work I heard that the producers thought the idea was great. This was the plan as it was laid out to me: "We'll tell fans we need 10,000 signatures by the end of week and then you'll jump into a giant pie."

And . . . go!

My co-host, Kevin Pereira, chimed in: "We'll get 10,000 signatures by the end of day. We have to make it more. It's not that exciting if it's an easy number to hit."

Kevin was right. In fact, by the end of the show that day, just an hour after we'd announced the petition, we'd already reached 10,000 signatures. So we decided to up the ante. If we could get 50,000 signatures by end of week, not only would I jump into a massive pie, but I would jump into a massive pie dressed as a French maid. The thinking was this—giant pies are delicious; French maids are sexy. Voila!

We scored over 60,000 signatures. There was a special French maid outfit made for me at Trashy Lingerie in Los Angeles. Commence palpitations.

To be honest, when we realized we were going to reach the number, I started to freak out. Cool—so I'm going to put on a patent leather French maid outfit and then jump into a ridiculously large pie . . . and then what? I just sit there like some stupid-ass chick who thinks she's hot and the audience loves me so much they'll just sit there watching me . . . sit . . . in pie? Ugh. I despise girls like that. But it was too late. I'd announced the petition and my plan. So how could I save myself from this?

"Kevin has to jump in with me," I blurted at a meeting. "And he has to wear a French maid outfit, too."

If I jumped in as a French maid it's dirty and sexy . . . and that's about it. But if Kevin put on the same outfit and jumped in with me? Well, now that's entertainment. Dirty, sexy entertainment.

Finally, it was jump day. We had, literally, cleared out all of the greater Los Angeles County area of its chocolate pie filling. (Yes, if you had gone happily to the market that day all excited to make a chocolate pudding pie only to find the shelves barren, blame me.) Everyone at work was all aflutter.

I've personally never used the phrase "all aflutter," but that is exactly how to describe it. There were people I'd never seen in our studio hanging around with anticipation. They apparently worked in sales and legal and the café. Even the president of G4 came down to witness the spectacle. It was intense and palpable and really fucking uncomfortable. There were photographers and press and an extra dose of enthusiasm among our producers, staff and crew that we only had on special occasions. It was like that feeling you get when it's field trip day in elementary school. Plus pie.

As I stood next to this giant pie—which by the way, looked ohmygodsogood!!—a producer pulled me aside and told me, "Okay . . . so you'll drop your robe and then *slowly* walk over to the ladder. When you get to the top, take your time. And then unbutton the top shirt *slowly* and really play it up. And then when you're ready, jump in."

Man, did I feel cheap.

I couldn't believe this was my goddamn idea. I was standing in a robe, with heels, garter panty hose and some lame lacy headband, and I was regretting every moment of it. I could see the crowd behind the cameras with all their own cameras, smiling and giggling.

"No," I responded to the producer's directions. "That's so stupid. There's no way I'm turning this into some strip show. That's just gonna make me look like an ass. I'm gonna be one of those girls who gets up trying to look sexy and thinking that that's good TV. It's not."

"But, Olivia. . . . that's what the fans want," the producer responded. "What else are you gonna do?"

"I have no idea. But, I'm not doing that," I said. "I'll just do whatever comes to me."

5, 4, 3 . . . We're live.

I drop the robe, smile, and stand on top of the pie, looking down about seven feet to its frothing surface. Kevin begins the countdown and suddenly it was a swirling combination of fun and regret. Somehow we managed to laugh at ourselves through the nerves.

And then I jumped. And I hit the bottom of the pie pan with a thud. I was promised that the pie filling was so thick, there was no way I would hit the bottom. (Who would even know that, by the way? Maybe some sort of pastry chef/ physicist that we didn't have on staff.) There was a single metal bar at the bottom of the pie and I managed to hit my shins directly on it, which actually takes some real skill. I winced with a pain that was so intense I thought I might pass out. I never really thought about it before, but I think when it's my time to go I actually would like to drown in pie. And then I remembered that I'm sitting . . . in a giant pie . . . dressed like a naughty French maid. And everyone is watching. Oh, hello! I couldn't just sit there crying. I shook off the pain and sat up. Which, it should be noted, is so not easy to do in a massive pie. Try it sometime.

The whole crowd was laughing and applauding and waiting for me to *do something*. Kevin leaned over with a

giant spoon and fed me some of the pie, the pie that surrounded me, my pie, and asked me how it was. The room
went very, very quiet, as everyone waited for my reaction.
Then I just went with it, did the only thing I could think that
made sense—I started splashing my hands in the chocolate pudding like a baby in a bath and burbled, "Om nom
nom nom nom!!!"

The crowd erupted again.

Of course I knew Kevin was going to jump into the pie
as French maid numero deux, just as soon as he ripped
off his tearaway tux. But in all the excitement I had forgot-
ten and when I heard the crowd cheer I turned around to
see him stripping down and I squealed with excitement.
(He looked surprisingly good in that French maid outfit.)
He jumped in, also hitting the metal bar of death, and the
crowd went even wilder. Like wild, pie-loving cheetahs
they went! In the end it made for great TV, the press loved
it and the ratings were huge. And Kevin and I didn't feel
cheap. We did it the way we wanted to do it. We had fun
and stayed true to our sensibilities and our humor.

Afterward, our dressing room showers looked like the
set of a snuff film directed by fucking Keebler elves. There
was chocolate pie filling smeared across the shower walls
and gathered in piles on the ground. Kevin had to jump into
a swimming pool later that night just to wash out all the
pudding lodged in his ears. I'd like to take this moment to

officially apologize to whomever was in charge of cleaning up our showers, because it had to have looked really scary in there.

The video and pictures of the pie jump were on about a million Web sites and blogs the next day. I had friends and coworkers and even studio heads e-mailing me about it. Most of the messages went something like, "Hey! Saw you jump into a pie? That was awesome."

In the end our petition, with its almost 70,000 signatures, wasn't enough (or maybe not important enough) to move the government to make it National Pie Week. What, like fixing health care is so important?! But it was a great week for us. And a great stunt. And I might even do it again . . . but probably not in the French maid outfit. How *do* they get any cleaning done in those things, anyway?

While I'm not totally sure why fans have connected so strongly with my love of pie I think it's partly because we live in a world where everyone on TV appears to be perfect and says their life is perfect and fans can't help but be envious and try to emulate their on-screen heroes. Not to sound too grand but I ripped up that veil and showed my belly and flaws and basically said it was all a facade. And then I jumped into an enormous chocolate pudding pie wearing a sexy French maid outfit.

It might not be Cassavetes but I'm proud of that moment. I'm proud that young girls out there can see a girl

who has hips, a butt, and some fat on her arms can get a chance to make it in Hollywood. And that even with the roundness of my belly and my carb-loaded lunches, I can still be asked to be on the cover of magazines. I can have my pie and eat it, too! And then have some more when no one is looking.

In interviews I'm often asked what I think about "being a sex symbol." And my answer is always: "That's very nice. And if people consider me sexy, I think it's great for young women to see a real woman, with real breasts and thick thighs considered sexy. I hope that changes the insanely narrow definition of sexy we generally see in the press and on television. Young girls should be proud of their imperfections and curves."

And then I think:

Suck it, skinny bitches!

chapter twenty-eight
random true story #3

Here's the scene:

I'm on the set of this horror movie, and I'm doing my first scene with an experienced Actor. The movie takes place inside an insane asylum and centers around a power-hungry doctor who was giving patients his own medical concoctions that end up turning the patients into flesh-eating zombies. It was a really fun movie to shoot and I loved my time on it. I especially love telling this little story.

Actor plays the creepy older doctor and I play the tired, but good-hearted nurse. In my first scene I'm attacked by a patient in a hallway and Actor walks in and saves me. End scene.

End scene? Not if you're Actor!

At the very end of the scene, he turns to me and says, "I should check your neck . . . meet me in the shower." CUT! The director runs up to us. "Great. Really great. Actor—let's try it again, but leave out the last line you added. Great!"

This was good advice, mostly because this line was not in the script.

And . . . action!

I'm choked by a patient. The doctor rescues me and says, "Meet me back in my office. I'll check your neck. You need a shower." CUT! The director runs up again. "Great. Really great. Actor—I think we need to leave the last line out. Your characters aren't dating."

Actor: "Nooooo. I think it would be great if my character and her character have a thing going on and then we cut to them in a shower and she can be wearing a white shirt."

Apparently it's true: all actors do want to direct. I'm standing there, eyes wide open, fumbling through my memory trying to remember where he read that in the script.

"Uuumm, yeah . . . Your characters aren't dating. And I

don't really think we need that," the director says. "So, let's just do it again—it's great—we'll just do it without that line."

Action!

Choked, doctor rescues me and . . . "I really should check your neck. Meet me in the shower."

Cut!

Damn.

!

The finished edit does not in fact have this line. From what I hear there was some clever editing to keep it out.

But, I gotta hand it to Actor. He had a vision for his character and he wasn't letting anyone stop him.

Just woulda been nice if we shared the same vision.

chapter twenty-nine
why i'd rather date a geek

Growing up in an

Air Force family, I moved around a lot. And yes, at times it was fucking hard. It's unbelievably difficult to walk into a new school where everyone has already clawed their way to a particular social status and try to be welcomed in. If you think of a new school as a lion's den and all the other students as bloodlusting lions who want only to sink their razor fangs into your flesh and rip and rip and rip, until a river of crimson has washed the whole world away, then you will have in mind a mild version of what I'm talking about. The reality is, as a new student coming into the lion's den, you are not always welcome.

And it's not about being a girl. Or that girls are more catty and protective of their circle and don't like other pretty girls or any of that stereotypical bullshit. The fact is, at that age, no one wants a new person to be added to their world. Especially if that new person could conceivably steal their boyfriend, innocence or Game Boy. If you've seen even one after-school special in your life, you understand exactly what I'm talking about. It's already hard enough to make it to whatever social class you've made it to, and then to have some new kid come in and possibly dethrone or replace you creates a lot of negative, nervous energy. That's like one of those rare New Age-y sounding ideas that also happens to be true—weird!

Whenever I'd go into a new school I would spend the first few months without any friends at all. Sure, this let me master my *Super Mario*, *Tetris,* and *Street Fighter* skillz, but still. Thankfully I had a sibling who went to the same school with me, so we would have each other to eat lunch with. Which, as we all know, is the most difficult part of the school day. Uuughh—I absolutely despised lunches or recesses. If it was regular class, there was a teacher and we all sat in our own assigned seats, listened to her and did our work. But now, out in the wild frontier of the playground or in the lunchroom wasteland where seats weren't assigned by alphabetical order, but by popularity, a flood of anxiety would wash over me. The unlucky ones were forced to eat by themselves or make new friends or *try* to make new friends. And then they got shot down by cooler kids. No thanks. I'd rather sit by myself. Hey, at least that way nobody would make fun of my lunch. Except my lunch—which does start talking to you if you've been alone long enough.

In fifth grade I moved to a new school and of course it all started over again. This was a period of my life where I wore all my hair on one side of my face, covering my eye and weighing my head down so it was always tilted to the left. I sat there in my new fifth-grade class and prayed for senior year to roll around. It couldn't come fast enough.

In fifth grade I moved to a new school and of course it all started over again.

Then one day a note was passed to me. And it read, "Will you go out with me? Jeremy." He was a boy with brown, spiky hair who wore glasses, striped Polo shirts, and braided belts. I actually didn't even know what his note meant. I didn't think about boys or dating or getting asked out. I folded the paper and put it in my awesome unicorn Trapper Keeper. At recess, Jeremy came up to me on the swings and asked me again, "Will you go out with me?" I responded, "Go where?" I honestly had no idea what he

was talking about. Like, outside? Or maybe to the super-market? No idea.

The other girls around me starting laughing and I sud-denly realized what he meant. He stood there by himself, no friends around, awkward and nerdy. And he was the only one, since the week that I'd been at this new school, who had said anything to me. He was a loner nerd and I was a loner new girl with weird fucking hair hiding my face. If it wasn't exactly love, it was better than nothing at all. I could almost hear the drum solo of our own personal power ballad.

We went on our first date to the mall and went to a Spencer's gift store and to the arcade. We didn't ex-change more than ten words all day. It was like a date with a mime. That was our only date and while Jeremy would never be confused for Han Solo or Leonardo DiCaprio, it was still awesome. Finally someone had been nice and sweet to me.

As I went through different schools and continued being the new girl there was always one thing I desperately wanted—to be in the popular group. Who didn't, right? That to me was the answer to all my problems. When you were in the popular group no one fucked with you, you al-ways had someone to eat lunch with and you had a team of classmates to cheat on tests with. The thought that I might be popular some day gave me something to shoot for; it was what I aspired for in every school. And Lord knows getting there was not going to be easy. But you know what? Through every school and state and country, the one group of kids I could always count on to be sweet and welcoming and let me eat lunch with them was the geeks.

After a few years of moving to new schools I stopped being afraid to be lonely. It took me a while but I finally realized that there would always be geeks. And geeks aren't concerned with being popular or making sure they're voted homecoming princess because their whole life they've been on the outside. And let me tell you, once you've been on the outside, you find out that it's actually pretty awesome out there. It's much easier to be yourself when nobody is watching . . . or better yet, you don't care if anybody is watching.

So why would I rather date a geek? Because they're who I relate to the most. They're the ones who always saved a seat for the new girl at the lunch table, or invited me to play Dungeons & Dragons in the computer lab at recess (when they needed the services of a halfling illusionist) instead of sitting in the shade by myself. (Like the good geek I was, I avoided the sun.) Because geeks are smart and passionate and really sweet people. And because geeks made me comfortable being myself and not feeling the need to conform.

I'm asked a lot if I'd ever date a geek. The answer is hell, yes. I'd prefer to date a geek. And let me be clear that the word "geek" today does not mean what it used to mean. A geek isn't the skinny kid with a pocket protector and acne. Being a geek just means that you're passionate about something. There can be computer geeks, video-game geeks, car geeks, military geeks, and sports geeks. Geeks are now sexy and empowered and strong and creative. I mean, just look at Bill Gates. Or the Google guys. Geeks are empowered and strong and creative. And that's sorta sexy, right?

So if you are you there, Geeks, it's me, Olivia. Would anyone like to come over and play *Call of Duty 4* with me? Or, if you'd rather, I'm sure I've got a twelve-sided dice somewhere around here.

chapter thirty

suck it, wonder woman!

When I started working

at G4 I thought I would be able to continue acting in other projects at the same time. And within the first six months of starting on *Attack of the Show!* I booked two different theatrical jobs. But because of my G4 time commitments, I wasn't able to take on the additional work. I started to become creatively frustrated and stunted. I was having a great time on *AOTS* and the ratings were fantastic. But I needed to do something else, too. I needed to become a different character and create something new for myself. That's what I love about acting— putting on a new persona, delving into a new world and just pretending. Or, alternately, putting on tights and gold, bullet-deflecting bracelets and letting 'er rip!

So, yes, I had an artistic void that needed to be filled. A creative itch that needed scratching. A performance bug that needed . . . swatting? An inspired vaginal condition that needed ointment.

Um, forget that last one.

Anyway, I decided to start doing skits for *Attack of the Show!*. This was around the same time that rumors were circulating that Wonder Woman was going to be made into a feature film. I called up G4's comic book expert and my close friend Blair Butler, and told her I'd love to do a skit about Wonder Woman and what it's like for her to be a *female* superhero—there are no pockets in your super-spandexy hot shorts, invisible jets are hard to find and the bad guys are always hitting on you.

We shot the Wonder Woman skit and it was so much fun. I put on the spandex starry shorts, red bustier, tall red boots and headgear. I felt . . . powerful and indestructible—I felt like a superhero! I felt badass enough that if I saw the real Wonder Woman I would've told her to suck it! It's funny how putting on a costume can completely change your state of mind and how you walk. I totally now understand how everyone looks forward to Comic-Con and dressing up. You feel invincible and strong and any social awkwardness you might normally have is hidden behind a mask . . . literally. Blair and I had a blast shooting the skit. I was running around, posing, being a badass saving peo-

ple . . . but eventually you do start to feel like you're becoming the character—and that's when trouble happens.
There was a fight scene where Blair dressed up as Chee-
tah and I had to take her down. I threw her to the ground
and the next thing I heard was a loud crack—it was Blair's
head hitting the concrete. Oh, shit. I completed the scene
and didn't let her injury ruin the shot. Because hey—it's already happened. Why ruin

**But now when I
shoot skits I'm much
more careful when I
bludgeon someone
to the ground.**

the shot and have to have
her do it again? And yes, I
would've stopped if she
screamed out in pain or
yelled "cut," but she didn't.
Thankfully, the cost for Blair
was just a small bump. But now when I shoot skits I'm
much more careful when I bludgeon someone to the
ground. In fact, we've come up with a safe word: Petunia.
When I hear that, I know we've got to stop immediately. Or
buy flowers. Luckily we've never had anyone use the safe
word . . . yet.

Now, little did I know at the time, but this was the beginning
of what would turn out to be my calling card on the network. Soon after the great response came back from the
network on that first skit, we created a master list of all the
geek icons that we could turn into a skit for me—Slave

Leia, the Baroness from *G. I. Joe*, Emma Frost from X-Men, Silk Spectre from *Watchmen*, Lara Croft, the Wonder Twins, and Catwoman, just to name a few.

I love doing these skits, but at some point it gets to be a little much. I mean, really, can someone answer this for me: Why are all female superheroes packed into spandex and hot shorts? Okay, of course I know the answer. I know why they're all scantily clad. It's because men draw them and if there is one thing men love it's boobs! And legs! And boobs! But really what they love is boobs.

The truth is, I actually dig the outfits. They're sexy and fun and I feel really fucking awesome in them. But, Jesus Christ, you can't eat for a good week before you put these things on. Not even pie. Sigh.

When I put on Wonder Woman, I didn't eat any carbs for a week (suck it in, Wonder Woman), didn't eat past 7 P.M. and did Pilates morning and night. I got a spray tan for the first time (first of many) and hated every second of it. When you get spray-tanned you are in a booth with a total stranger and you get completely naked. It's like Times Square in the seventies. As she sprays you with the cold dark liquid, you can see the tan land on your skin. It's as if you're getting painted. I call it "getting dipped" because that's what it feels like. Like you are just a giant human ice-cream cone getting dipped in delicious caramel dipping sauce. Holy crap, I'm hungry.

And then there's the bustier. Contrary to popular belief (and what you see thanks to the magic of Photoshop), I don't have very large breasts. I actually created my own bra that specializes in giving you amazing cleavage, especially when you wouldn't normally have it. I created this bra on the set of the Wonder Woman skit. Because when I first put on that bustier I noticed how sad my boobs looked, how very un-Wonderful they looked, and how powerful the outfit was. Didn't really match, you know? So I fashioned my own bra. I'd love to tell you exactly how I created my bra, but I can't. Trade secrets, bitches! Because I'm in the middle of creating and patenting it as you read this. But I promise, for the next book, I'll give out a free bra with every book you buy. Deal? So I invented a bra and my boobs have never been the same. Some mornings they thank me and other days they just scream at me and cry, "Just leave us alone! We're not meant to be pushed up so goddamn high! We need a break. Just one day of relief." Which reminds me, I have got to get back to listening to my *How to Speak Boob in Five Weeks or Less* tapes.

Now for something a little bit unpleasant: the hot shorts. Every girl hates her ass. It's true. And I am no different. Except that no girl hates her ass as much as a girl whose ass is packed into a Wonder Woman costume. So here was the scene: Me, hating my ass, in full Wonder Woman gear and hot shorts. Running. (Despite how horrible I'm making it sound now, it is actually one of my favorite outfits. And I hope to one day put it into the Smithsonian . . . or at the very least be able to wear it when I'm eighty. Sorry for that visual. Old lady ass in hot shorts is generally not a pretty image.) In short, I could've used the assistance of another superhero: Magical Ass-Slimming Man.

This is difficult to admit out loud, but one outfit that I actually 100 percent regret is the Slave Leia outfit. I know it's a surprise that I regret it because the pics have gone everywhere and a lot of people seemed to really like it.

Here's what happened. We were going to shoot a *Highlander* skit at the *Star Wars* 30th Anniversary Celebration. I had my outfit specially made for me and it was very expensive. And rad. Before a shoot like this I usually diet for at least three days to look as lean as possible. But for this one, I guess I was just having one of those weeks and I thought to myself, "Whatever, you look fine. Just eat what you want." Big mistake. Big, big, enormous, jeans-busting mistake. When I shoot a skit in our studios, it's a controlled environment and I know where the camera is at all times. I know how to position my body for an angle and how to yell at someone for taking a picture of my ass. (Note: like this— "Don't take a picture of my ass!")

But when you're in a public setting, with massive amounts of fans, and you're dressed as the sexiest character of that genre in barely anything, you DO NOT get photo approval over everyone's cameras at the event. Ipso facto or whatever, there were pictures of me from every angle, and not all of them were flattering. When people tell me I'm being silly for thinking that and that I "looked great," I tell them they're wrong. Then I yell: "Don't take a picture of my ass!" So that's why I have vowed to never wear the Slave Leia outfit in public again. And most likely not even for a skit. Sorry, but I just can't do it. Hey, you try putting on a gold bikini and hang out with Jabba the Hut. It's no picnic. It's not even a light snack.

The Lesbionic Woman was a fun one to shoot with less anxiety because I was fully dressed for that skit. The premise of the skit is a parody on *The Bionic Woman,* but instead of bionic, she becomes faster, stronger, and incredibly good at munching female muff. In the skit you see me wake up and, realizing I've become lesbionic, I begin to fight crime with my lady powers. I save the world by making out with the female assassin and my kiss is so powerful she caves in right away.

Before we did that shoot, the producer asked if I wanted to cast the girl to kiss, or if I knew someone I was comfortable kissing. The only person I could think of was my spray-tan lady. She wanted to be an actress and she saw me naked all the time anyway, so I thought it was perfect.

I'll help her out and she'll make me less nervous. Plus—discounted spray tans for life!

I'd never kissed a girl before on camera and was not really looking forward to this one. Not that there's anything wrong with it or with my spray-tan lady, it's just not something I've ever wanted to do. And it probably didn't help that my spray-tan lady was really excited about the scene and told me how she practiced with friends.

(I will pause here while you run to your computer, search for the video and possibly rub one out and/or consider hooking up with your own spray-tan lady. Ready to continue? Great.)

So we went in for the kiss and it was so . . . glossy. Just totally glossy. Two girls, both wearing a shit-ton of lipgloss. And, I'm sorry to report, it wasn't very nice. She was a good kisser, but all that gloss just made it gross. It was like kissing a Slip 'n Slide that had dressed for a night out. Perhaps you'd like me to say that it was amazing and we went home and finger-banged each other. And, sure, that would be hot in a way. But, sadly, what you see in the Lesbionic skit is as far as I took it. But hey, at least I saved the world.

The last thing I will say on all this costumery for now is that dressing up as a superhero is surprisingly hard. But despite all the working out, tanning, makeup, special bras, not eating and spandex . . . it's also pretty fucking cool. I mean, there aren't many jobs around where you get to beat up bad guys while wearing go-go boots. (And, no, vigilante stripper does not count.) So it's just too bad for me that being Wonder Woman is not a real vocational possibility (it's not, right?). Guess I'll just have to settle for the next best thing—dressing up *like* Wonder Woman, crushing fake fools to dust and shouting intimidating smack at anyone who dares cross my path.

Stuff like: Don't take a picture of my ass! And: Suck it, Wonder Woman!

chapter thirty-one
how to make love like a zombie

As I sit writing this—

in late 2009—there is perhaps no scary creature as hot as zombies, though Glenn Beck is certainly giving the undead a run for their money. Zombies are hot at the movies, hot in books and hot on our trail—gotta go! I kid, but not really. That is actually part of the appeal of zombies, I think: they seem like they could exist. Unlike vampires, who may or may not come from Transylvania and speak with absurd accents, and werewolves, who would never survive in warm climates under all that fur, zombies could be real; they are, in many ways, just us— with terrible skin. And gimpier walks. And an unyielding, unceasing, absolutely all-consuming desire to eat brains. But otherwise, they are just like us. And if that's the case, then shouldn't we be able to learn something from them? Call me crazy but I think so. And in considering what zombies could teach us, let's go for something big—something about life or money or death. Or love. Yes, love, let's go with love! Now that I think about it, zombies really could teach us something about the lovemaking arts. Sure, they may not always be that easy on the eyes but in the way that they live their lives (or whatever it is the undead do), there are a few excellent lessons we can all remember when it comes time to Make Love Like a Zombie.

BE A GREAT LISTENER. Communication is so incredibly important if you are interested in becoming an accomplished lover. And if you've seen so much as one scene from a George Romero movie then you know that nobody is as devoted to paying attention as zombies. Without their unflinching desire to attain a goal, the villains in *Night of the Living Dead* would never have been able to satisfy their monomaniacal urges. Think about that the next time you engage an object d'amour in spine-tinglingly deep conversation over dinner. The great news is that you don't need to have gone through a face-ravaging toxic accident to also excel in this department. The key is to lock in on your partner with zombielike intensity. That can, of course, be hard to do in this multitasking, highly-distracting, tweet-packed world we live in, but it can be done. You simply must tune out all the white noise that threatens to disrupt your intimate hours with your lover. Be present. You will thank me and, more important, your lover will thank me, especially if you can also give such single-minded attention to . . . *down there.*

GO SLOW. You know how most zombies walk at such a slo-mo molasses pace that it's a minor miracle they can catch even one victim? Well, apply that same principle to honoring and pleasuring your lover and s(he) will never forget you. I have read the statistics and so I know that women overwhelmingly say that they would like to have more foreplay involved in their lovemaking sessions. In other words—don't be all vampiric and go straight for the neck; sloooooow it down to zombie speed, bro. I know what you are thinking: But if I go too slowly, won't I miss some opportunities to party down? Of course you won't! Haven't you seen the creep-along orgy that is the original *Dawn of the Dead*? Those brain-suckers ambled so ridiculously slowly, you'd think they would've sprouted moss. And yet, they all totally nailed their target. And you will, too, if you take the time to explore each and every nook and valley of your lover's rocky physical terrain. Think of your partner's body as a postapocalyptic wasteland of scorched and still-smoldering Earth and treat it like a ravenous zombie who's dead-set on fulfilling its every bloody desire. Sexy!

FONDLE THEIR BRAINS. As any good zombie can tell you, brains are not just for breakfast, anymore. The brain, as the saying goes, can be the largest erogenous zone on a human body. So once again the undead were ahead of the lovemaking curve by placing so much emphasis on brains. The only error zombies make, as far as I can tell, is that they spend too much time trying to *eat*

...brains are not just for breakfast anymore.

brains and not enough time *stimulating* them. How you choose to stroke and stoke your lover's cerebrum is, of course, up to you, but there are a handful of ways I've found to turn on the top light. Phone sex, for example, is all about titillating your special someone's imagination, which is just another way of saying you are giving him or her a brain erection—or "brection."

A road less traveled might be to bake your lover a pie. This might sound odd at first, but I think you will be pleased by the effects of the wafting aroma of warm apples baking. Again, this will tease and arouse the brain that's connected to the body whose bones you wish to jump. Also—pie is delicious! Just don't combine thoughts here and bake them a brain pie because that is not so delicious, unless you really are a zombie. Which I am not. Swear!

chapter thirty-Two
location, location, etc.

These are all times

when life was so crazy and weird, you just really needed to be there . . .

When I was in fourth grade, one day I was sitting in class taking a test after lunch. I couldn't concentrate on the test because I had to pee so bad. I know the logical grown-up response would be that I could just get up and go to the bathroom. But at nine years old, I didn't want to get up in front of everyone and walk to the bathroom. I also didn't want the teacher to think I was cheating by leaving in the middle of a test.

So, I did the next best thing. I tried to let just a little pee out. Just a little so there'd be relief. Yes I was going to let myself pee *just a little bit* in my pants.

Did you know that it's very hard to just let a *little* pee out? Because once you need to go and you let yourself, it doesn't really stop.

So, I sat there, completely relieved, in the middle of class, in my own pee.

"No, I didn't pee my pants. Geez... I had *ice* in my pocket and it's melting ... duh."

The girl sitting next to me notices a drip coming from my chair and whispers, "Hey . . . hey . . . did you pee your pants?"

I felt instant panic. I don't know why I didn't think that anyone would notice. I didn't know what to do. I couldn't be the girl who *peed her pants!* So, I thought quickly and said, "No, I didn't pee my pants. Geez . . . I had *ice* in my pocket and it's melting . . . duh."

Yeah, child wonder over here went with the most logical answer—I was keeping *ice* in my *pockets*. The best part? To the best of my recollection, I'm pretty sure I felt confident she believed me. God, I'm an idiot.

★　★　★

There was a great deal on peaches at the grocery store down the street from my studio—a box of sixteen peaches for only $5.99. I thought it would be nice to get six boxes for the writers, producers and crew. I parked my car, ran inside the store and paid the cashier for six boxes. I went back to my car and drove it to the front of the store where all the peaches were stacked up. I jumped out of my car and raced around to start piling the peaches into my passenger side. Before I even pick up the first box, some woman pulled up behind me, got out of her car and screamed, "Can you move your car so I can get around?" It had seriously been less than ten seconds that I'd been stopped. I smiled and yelled back, "Yep, right away. I just prepaid for these peaches and I'm gonna throw them in my car real quick!" I grabbed the boxes two at a time to be fast. Before I could even get the first two boxes in my car, the woman, still standing outside her car yelled out again, "Seriously! Am I on *Candid Camera* or something?!"

It had been a total of maybe forty-five seconds since I stopped my car! I put down the peaches, looked at her (this time not smiling), thought about how dumb and outdated that sarcastic quip was and then responded, "Yes. Yes, you are on *Candid Camera*. And you might wanna fix your hair and face 'cause you look like shit."

She just dropped her mouth open in shock and got back in her car. It was so awesome.

*　*　*

A friend of mine lost her job and asked if she could move to Los Angeles and work as my assistant. She said she saw how busy my life had become and would be happy to help me out. So, I gave my current assistant time to find another

job and then hired my best friend.

People always say "don't mix business and friendship." But they never say *why*. I'll tell you why. Because when you inevitably ask them to do a favor for you as a friend like, oh I don't know, "hand me that glass please," they think you should be paying them for that.

She was the worst assistant somehow managing to do things completely backwards and would end up costing me double.

But one day we found her calling! She loves gardening and offered to water my hedges and take care of them. That's great! That'll save me a little money on a gardener each week. Awesome.

One day I came home and she said with a smile, "I need $300." I asked what it was for. Her response? "Oh! I had sprinklers installed so we don't have to water the hedges anymore!"

Seriously?! So we don't have to water the hedges?!! Bitch, your ass said you were gonna water them! So, you offered to water the hedges to save me money, but instead installed sprinklers that *I* had to pay for, so now *you* don't have to water them. Wow. You're either a fucking genius, or a bad friend. Oh, man—you really needed to be there.

★   ★   ★

A few years back I dated a guy for a year and then one day we broke up. Later on, through mutual friends, I found out that he had been cheating on me. Years went by before I finally ran into him again. I guess he got some kind of spark when he saw me and called me later that week.

"I wanted to see if I could take you to dinner tonight."

"Yeah, I don't think so," I responded.

"Why not?" he asked.

"Because I don't really want to start anything with you again," I said.

"Why not? We were so great together. Let's give it another shot. I'd love to be with you again, So, why not?" he said.

"Why not? Okay. Because the entire time we were together you never made me come. Not once. I faked it for almost a whole year. And I really don't want to fake it anymore."

That was 100 percent true. And I'd wanted to say that for a long time. He was speechless and it felt good. Perhaps you needed to be there.

chapter thirty-three
FAQ for a supergeek

1. What color would your Lightsaber be?

OM: It would be a color you could only see if you were wearing special Olivia Lightsaber glasses. That way my enemy would never see it coming. And the color that you would see through the glasses would be called "Spearmint Fuck-Yeah" just because I think that's an awesome name for a color.

2. If you could have any superpower, what would it be, and why?

It's a typical answer, but I would really love to be able to fly. I dream about flying almost every night. I'm usually getting chased and the only way to escape is to fly. And for some reason I fly like Super Mario Brothers with a running start. I think about flying all the time. I am obsessed with squirrel jumping. (Look it up.) I know it's intense and really dangerous but I want to try it one day.

3. What's the funniest thing you've ever seen at Comic-Con?

A guy dressed as Darth Vader making out with Princess Leia. I mean, come on, that's just not realistic.

4. What is your favorite video-game console ever?

Xbox 360. There are so many great games for it.

5. Favorite song to play on *Guitar Hero*?

Anything by Journey.

6. A criminal mastermind kidnaps you—what comic book hero would you want coming to your rescue?

Superman. Because there's only one thing that could stop him. And let's face it—it's really hard to get kryptonite.

7. If you had to pick one *Lord of the Rings* character to escort you to Mount Doom, whom would you take (one does not simply *walk* into Mordor!)?

I would take Sam. Because going into Mount Doom is a death wish. And if I'm gonna die, I'd like to have a good laugh before I go, and Sam makes me laugh the most.

8. Would you rather own a jetpack or a Tesla coil?
Jetpack. (See: all that stuff about flying.)

9. What is your favorite mythological beast (centaur, minotaur, dragon, etc)?
Dragon. Because if I could tame a dragon, I could ride him around and fly. (Yes, I'm obsessed with flying.)

10. How would you survive a zombie apocalypse?
I would get a group of ten people, taking no children or elderly, and we would barricade ourselves in my basement, which is already zombie-ready (because how stupid are you if you haven't already started preparing?), and wait it out until the zombies took down the city and went on to the next. Then, when they thought we were dead, we would follow them into the next town and take them down when they least expect it. We would begin to hunt them. And then of course, decapitate them, because that's how you kill zombies.

256

Which Is Cooler:

11. *Super Mario* or *Zelda*?
Super Mario.

12. *Pacman* or *Tetris*?
Tetris all the way. I'm like a prodigy, fourteen years too late.

13. Ninjas or pirates?
Ninjas.

14. *Battlestar Galactica* or *Firefly*?
BSG.

15. *A New Hope* or *The Empire Strikes Back*?
The Empire Strikes Back.

16. *Raiders of the Lost Ark* or *The Last Crusade*?
Raiders of the Lost Ark.

17. Macs or PCs?
Mac for daily Internet use. PC for gaming.

In these hypothetical situations, what would you do?

18. You find a Magic Hat of Infinite Endurance and

now you no longer require sleep. How do you
spend all your extra free time?

*Eating pie and working off the pie I just ate.
That and organizing my house and all of my
friends' homes—I have OCD.*

19. You wake up one day to find that scientists
have cloned you. Olivia Munn #2 is your exact
copy in every way. What will you do with your new
clone?

*Kill her. A clone is a great idea in theory. But,
eventually she will get jealous of me and turn
on me. It won't be good. But, I'd make it quick
and painless. After all, it is me.*

20. Your favorite movie director calls you up. He
wants to cast you in a big summer blockbuster, to
play a comic book heroine of your choice. Would
you accept, and whom would you want to play?

*Hell yes. And I would be Wonder Woman, or
Jayna from the Wonder Twins.*

21. You're alone on a desert island. Or so you
think. It's actually swarming with velociraptors. You
have only seconds before they pick up your scent.

What to do?

Start swimming.

22. Question #19 was a trap. Your clone is actually a Cylon, which you discover one day when you spot Olivia Munn #2 flirting with your Roomba. You can only assume that a massive robot invasion draws nigh, the fate of the human race resting in your hands . . . but whom can you trust?

Aha! Well, good thing I killed her! Then when I see my Roomba acting up, I call Shia LeBeouf and ask for his help in destroying the world . . . or just make out with him before surrendering to the robots.

23. Your ninja dojo is shamed when a rival clan ambushes your sensei, taking him hostage. While in the midst of planning a rescue mission you get a call from Master Splinter. He has learned of your situation and can spare one (but only one) of the Teenage Mutant Ninja Turtles to assist you. Splinter is waiting for your response.

No thanks. I'm gonna go this alone. But please send some extra pizza.

24. You have an opportunity to make out with a shape-shifting wizard whom you find moderately attractive. Halfway through, there's an 82 percent chance that he will turn into the hottest man ever, a 15 percent chance that he will turn into the ugliest woman ever, and a 3 percent chance that he will turn into a man-eating tiger.

No guy is worth those chances. I decide not to make out with him and get a mani-pedi instead.

chapter thirty-four

"if you can get friction with that tuba, you deserve a 25-year-old girlfriend."

Just a week before

I was going to be on *Late Night with Jimmy Fallon*
I had a massive panic attack. How massive?
Well, I blacked out and woke up on my living
room floor with no one around and went to the
hospital thinking I was having a severe asthma
attack. That massive. After being hooked up to
machines, having a tube down my throat to keep
me from choking since my throat was literally
closing up, and having numerous tests done, the
doctor comes in and tells me I'm having a panic
attack. The worst she's ever seen. And if I didn't
go home and rest and shut my body down, I was
at risk of having a heart attack! A heart attack?
Isn't that something old fat guys who eat greasy
sandwiches for lunch every day get?

I was shocked. Mentally I was fine. And everything in my life was going great. But as the doctor told me, panic attacks can come when there's bad *and* good in your life. My body was dealing with a lot and it just had had enough.

I called in to work and slept all day long. And I continued to sleep for basically three more days. On the fourth day, I felt rested and back to normal. Whew—a huge relief.

Then, the day came to appear on *Fallon* and as I was sitting in makeup I felt my chest tightening and my throat closing up. No, no, no. This cannot happen now. I was so excited to be on the show and it was kind of a big deal for me and it would not be cool to get a panic attack just hours before it.

But fuck—it was not stopping. My breathing was getting shallow and my palms were sweating. I had performed on television for thousands of hours and had never had a problem—why was this happening now?

I finally realized why my panic attack was coming up—I was nervous. When I tell people I get nervous before things like this or in front of audiences, they're always surprised. I know I have a big personality on air, but the truth is I always get nervous. Most of the time, my nerves calm down as soon as I step on stage. Other times, they don't.

But for *Fallon*, there was something specific that was making me uneasy and once I figured it out, I could handle it better. I had to get all spiritual on my own ass and look inward. So that's what I did.

And I realized I was dealing with two conflicting emotions: be funny and don't be funny. Of course I wanted to be funny and make everyone laugh. I really wanted that. But at the same time, I just wanted to be myself and not be "on" so people could get to know my personality better when it wasn't cranked to ten. So, there I was, about to go do a huge late-night talk show on NBC and I wasn't sure how to be funny and how not to be funny. Or, really, how funny was the right amount of funny. This may sound simple but it really isn't. For one thing, being funny is pretty damn hard. To measure it out like baking powder in a recipe for fruity muffins is really tricky. And on top of that, you never know how the audience will react to you. They could totally get your sense of humor and love you, or think you're not entertaining or likeable and give you nothing. You just never know. And so—nerves!

My makeup artist, publicist, a friend and I pulled up to the front of 30 Rock in midtown Manhattan where they tape the show and there was a large group of fans waiting to take pictures and get an autograph. I always take time with the fans and really enjoy that part of being a performer, but I guess I was running late because a large man pushed people away and whisked me through to a private elevator. I felt like Shakira . . . or some still-relevant superstar.

When we get to the dressing room, it was this fantastic little room with great style, including tiny little video games

decorating the walls. There was a tray of amazing cup-
cakes, a veggie platter and a gift bag with the softest
T-shirt ever made inside. I'm not kidding: this T-shirt was,
like, made from the testicles of baby lambs or something.

My makeup artist set up to touch me up, my publicist
was asking me a bunch of questions, and a cameraman
and producer were shooting behind the scenes for the G4
network. The room, though awesome, was also the size of
a closet. There were way too many people in there. It was
getting hot and not in the Nelly way (Yay, late '90s refer-
ence!). I could feel my panic attack coming on stronger
than ever.

I kicked everyone out of the room and took ten minutes
to just breathe by myself. I was not gonna let myself pass
out on national television . . . especially not in my short-ass
dress.

It's funny: whenever you tell people you need a minute
by yourself, everyone assumes you didn't mean *them*.
Knock, knock and . . . a walk-in. Knock, knock and . . . a
head-poke in. Knock, knock and . . . a need-anything request. You're truly never left alone at these things. I was like
the president in a short-ass dress about to black out cold
from panic, except instead of having something important
to say or do that would impact the entire world, I just had to
do my first late-night talk show.

The producer of the show walked in and we started to

go through my questions. I told him how nervous I was and he, too, was surprised by my anxiety. I explained that I'm nervous because I wanted to do a good job. That's it. I just wanted to do a good job. And as simple as that sounds, it's a lot harder to do. To just be yourself in front of a studio audience with a band playing and lights and cameras . . . it's hard. I started picturing a different life—one where I was a mellow sheepherder living in Mongolia with my family. I would walk with a staff and eat stew for dinner. I would not go on television.

I snapped back to reality. The producer and I walked through it enough times that I began to feel comfortable and then just when I needed one more minute to compose myself, someone grabbed me and walked me to a curtain. Within mere moments that same someone touched my shoulder and told me to walk through the curtain and . . . I'm there.

My nerves didn't go away instantly. But I was able to acknowledge they were there, deal with them, and just be present.

Oh, and did I mention who was also on the show that night? Artie Lange. Yep, from the Howard Stern show. I met Artie once and he was a great guy. He actually talked about meeting me on his show the next day and for one morning I was a hero to all my guy friends who listen religiously to Howard and Artie. "Ohmygod, Olivia! Artie's talking about you on Howard!"

Artie is a great, sweet, funny, lovable guy. But he has been known to often "take over" interviews. Not in a malicious way. Just in the way that he's a comedian and when he sees an in to make a joke, he takes it . . . and can do that over and over. I've seen him do it with other people. And I was warned he might do that on *Fallon* that night, but I wasn't worried at all. I wasn't worried about anyone. My anxiety was the only thing that could do me in. Unfortunately, my anxiety was proving to be like a 285-pound cage-match champion.

But then something beautiful happened. I'm not quite sure at what point in the interview this happened exactly, but my nerves just fell away. I just sat back and had fun being in the moment with Jimmy and Artie. All anxiety vanished.

I knew with my first joke that the audience got my sense of humor. Jimmy had asked if I liked technology, or if it was just something I talk about on my show. I responded with, "Yeah, I like technology. I mean, I have a computer." And when the audience laughed, I think that's probably when my nerves released their hold on me.

Later in the show, Artie made a joke about being on ecstasy and "banging that tuba," pointing in the direction of

The Roots, Jimmy's house band. The whole audience cracked up. And while they were laughing I looked over at the tuba with this massive hole in it and thought to myself, "Well, Artie did say his girlfriend was twenty-five . . . maybe he's got something going on." But instead of internalizing that comment, I turned to Artie and said, "Artie, if you can get friction with that tuba, you deserve a twenty-five-year-old

"Artie, if you can get friction with that tuba, you deserve a 25-year-old girlfriend."

girlfriend." The audience erupted in laughter. And Artie was practically speechless—well, as close to speechless as he ever gets—screaming, "Nice! Nice!" over and over, and Jimmy was out of his seat jokingly telling everyone to calm it down.

After the show Artie came up to Jimmy and me and said, "She had the best line of the night. That friction line was hilarious."

I was so happy. As entertainers and comedians I respect both Jimmy and Artie so much (not to mention the king of New York comedy himself, Lorne Michaels, who I had passed in the greenroom right before the show.) And to know that I had made them laugh and I'd surprised them, was a high I had a hard time coming down from. It was beyond what I dreamed it could be.

During the commercial breaks producers and executives had been running down to the set saying this was the best show they'd ever had. And Jimmy came to my room later and said, "There are shows that you dream and wish to have, but you never think you can get them. This was that show."

It was, in a word, amazing.

I hate to write out every moment of the show because that would be too grandiose. But I can say it was up there as one of the best moments of my life. I'm gonna say Top-3 best moments of my life.

The show ended with Jimmy and me playing Ping-Pong and I brought out my "secret partner"—Susan Sarandon. Yes. Susan Fucking Sarandon. I swear this is true: just days before Jimmy's show we had dinner for the first time and became fast friends. Jimmy had asked her to play Ping-Pong on his show in the past, but she declined because of a hurt wrist. But Susan co-owns a Ping-Pong club called SPiN in New York City and we had been practicing there together. The Ping-Pong game was between Susan and me and Artie and Jimmy. And it was not staged at all—other than the fact that Susan forced Jimmy to use a ridiculously small paddle. It probably goes without saying on this fairy-tale evening, but Susan and I brought the win home! What. Up.

I have to say I'm very happy we won that game. Because if you watch the match, I gave up the second point when I hit the ball off the table. When I did that, Susan said to me under her breath, "Come on! You can't hit like that." The fear of disappointing my new best friend, Susan Fucking Sarandon, was enough to get me focused and help us house Jimmy and Artie. We went back to SPiN that night and had a celebratory dinner and more Ping-Pong. I mean, really, what a goddamn perfect night!

I usually keep my head down and even when something good happens for me, I look up briefly, and throw my head back down. I guess I feel like if I keep it up too long, I'll get hit by a bus or something and it'll all go away. But this time, for this show, I let myself be excited and, dare I say, proud about how I handled it.

It's rare moments like this, when I allow myself to be excited about how life is turning out . . . and I think back to the little Olivia who just wanted to make people laugh so much—the one with the ridiculous Disney outfits, the one who had to bribe her "friends" to let her be the dog who stayed outside while playing house, the one who once tried desperately to fit into any clique that would have her. It's moments like this where I wish I could tell her: It's all gonna turn out fine.

Acknowledgments

I would never have

been able to get this book done without the following people and I would like to thank them all very much for everything they did to make it possible: My mom, my sister Sara—basically my whole family, Michael Homler, everyone at St. Martin's, Chris Scheina, Jon Favreau, Stan Lee, Masi Oka, Mac Montandon, Simon Green, and all the writers, producers, and crew from G4, Kevin Pereira, Neal Tiles, John Rieber, Dave Fleming, and Tim Kessler. And I also want to thank all my girlfriends with a few phrases that will make sense to no one except them. Really, one of the greatest accomplishments a woman can make is having amazing girlfriends. Here's to you guys:

- WWPND?
- I don't really want to talk right now.
- Toast
- Namaste
- Jam
- Sidestep
- Classic Newman
- Well, has he ever saved Middle Earth?
- Boys got the bullets but girls got the guns . . . but you don't need no stinkin' bullets if you know how to pistol whip a motherfucker.

CPSIA information can be obtained at www.ICGtesting.com
Printed in the USA
LVOW07s0759161214

419038LV00005B/568/P

9 780312 583767